An EasyGuide to
Research Presentations

An EasyGuide to Research Presentations

Janie H. Wilson
Georgia Southern University

Beth M. Schwartz
Randolph College

Los Angeles | London | New Delhi
Singapore | Washington DC

Los Angeles | London | New Delhi
Singapore | Washington DC

FOR INFORMATION:

SAGE Publications, Inc.
2455 Teller Road
Thousand Oaks, California 91320
E-mail: order@sagepub.com

SAGE Publications Ltd.
1 Oliver's Yard
55 City Road
London EC1Y 1SP
United Kingdom

SAGE Publications India Pvt. Ltd.
B 1/I 1 Mohan Cooperative Industrial Area
Mathura Road, New Delhi 110 044
India

SAGE Publications Asia-Pacific Pte. Ltd.
3 Church Street
#10-04 Samsung Hub
Singapore 049483

Printed in the United States of America.

Library of Congress Cataloging-in-Publication Data

Wilson, Janie H.

An easyguide to research presentations / Janie H. Wilson, Georgia Southern University, Beth M. Schwartz, Randolph College.

pages cm
Includes bibliographical references and index.

ISBN 978-1-4522-9267-0

1. Public speaking—Handbooks, manuals, etc.
2. Self-presentation—Handbooks, manuals, etc.
I. Schwartz, Beth M. II. Title.

PN4121.W453 2014
001.4'2—dc23   2013042698

This book is printed on acid-free paper.

Acquisitions Editor: Reid Hester
Editorial Assistant: Lucy Berbeo
Production Editor: David C. Felts
Copy Editor: Michelle Ponce
Typesetter: C&M Digitals (P) Ltd.
Proofreader: Pam Suwinsky
Indexer: Maria Sosnowski
Cover Designer: Gail Buschman
Marketing Manager: Shari Countryman

Certified Chain of Custody
Promoting Sustainable Forestry
www.sfiprogram.org
SFI-01268

SFI label applies to text stock

14 15 16 17 18 10 9 8 7 6 5 4 3 2 1

Contents

Preface

We decided to write this *EasyGuide* to help you, the student. And when we say "student," we mean anyone at any level who wants to learn more about sharing research with the world. We wanted to create one place for information on how to present research in poster or oral format, submit a manuscript for publication, and even create video presentations for later viewing. Sure, you could find the information in many locations, but who has time to pull together chapters, articles, websites, webpages, blogs, tweets, etc.? And we wanted to focus on research presentations rather than public speaking in general. A research presentation is a specific part of our research culture, and the culture has many expectations—both spoken and unspoken. In this book, we let you in on all the secrets, even explaining how to overcome stress, how to prepare for conference attendance, and what you should do (and not do) at a conference. We trust that everything you need to know about professional research presentations is located in this *EasyGuide*. If not, please contact us with your advice, comments, and suggestions. Or just contact us to say you love the book.

The book is divided into five sections, beginning with a section to orient you to the book as well as the idea of presenting your research. Chapter 1 explains our goals in more detail than this preface and offers encouragement to take the important step of presenting your research. Chapter 2 offers many ways to overcome (or at least reduce) anxiety that you might feel. Chapter 3 describes in detail how to choose a conference, pick the type of presentation you want to give, and submit a proposal. In this chapter we also provide timelines to help you prepare well in advance—and reduce stress!

In the second section of this book, Poster Presentations, we provide two chapters filled with step-by-step instructions on how to prepare a top-notch poster. In Chapter 4 you will read about the content of a poster based on numerous examples we have seen and created. Chapter 4 also provides instructions on how to create a poster in PowerPoint, including adding text boxes and details found in professional posters. In Chapter 5 we discuss adding visual interest to your poster; relevant information beyond text will draw people to your work. In this chapter we also cover how to create various types of graphs to communicate efficiently and effectively.

In the third section of this book, we offer many ways to create and deliver oral presentations. In Chapter 6 we explain how to build an oral presentation in PowerPoint. Chapter 7 covers Prezi presentations, which are gaining popularity as an alternative to PowerPoint. Chapter 8 details how to create an oral presentation using Keynote, an option for those who prefer Mac products. Chapters 6 through 8 carefully build presentations using a step-by-step approach that we hope removes any mystery surrounding the creation of oral-presentation materials. Finally, in Chapter 9 we explain how to prepare for actually giving your oral presentation, including the pace and volume of your talk, as well as how to win over your audience.

In the fourth section of this book, we offer advice based on many years of experience presenting our work at conferences and working with students to present their work. In Chapter 10 we discuss what to pack if you are going out of town, how to prepare for the conference (or class presentation) to enhance performance, and even what to avoid when preparing for your presentation. Chapter 11 offers important information about what will be expected of you on the day of your presentation, dividing expectations into posters and talks. This chapter also covers what you should expect from others and how the conference environment will look. The day after your presentation is important as well, and Chapter 12 explains the follow-up work you should do as a professional. Instead of presenting at a conference or in the classroom, you may find yourself needing to communicate your work, but for some reason you must archive the talk and let people watch it later.

The fifth section of this book offers advice on how to share you work with a broader audience. Chapter 13 provides detailed information about how to video your talk in case you need an asynchronous alternative. A video can be posted on YouTube or shared in many other ways with anyone you choose. As an added bonus, a video can be archived and viewed for a limitless time. Although a video offers flexible sharing, the best way to make your research widely available is to publish it in a professional journal. Chapter 14 explains in detail how to consider publishing your work, what is expected at every step of the submission process, and what you can expect to see and do after a decision is made by the editorial team. To make your life easier, we also offer sample letters that you might write and explain approaches when responding to reviewers' comments.

As you read *An EasyGuide to Research Presentations* and hopefully apply our advice to your own presentation, consider using the appendices to fine-tune your work. Appendix A offers checklists to keep you on track when preparing posters or talks. Appendix B provides assessment rubrics; carefully assessing your work can help to improve your presentation and increase your comfort and confidence.

Let us end this preface to the book with some encouragement. It has been our experience that students find the full research process to be taxing and exhilarating at the same time. Our students are amazed by what they can accomplish, and they beam with pride when they are able to share their work with others. With this book, our goal is to remove the stress of not knowing what to do next or how to do it. This book will provide the details needed to help you perform the final step in the research process, a step that allows you to share your findings with others. We love working with students and teachers, and we have a deep appreciation for sharing research. We trust *An EasyGuide to Research Presentations* will help you become an engaging, effective, proud member of the scientific community.

Acknowledgements

We are honored to work with so many dedicated students. After many years of teaching, we remain grateful for student input and positive interactions. We are also grateful for the amazing colleagues we have had during our careers, and we know the future holds many more cherished relationships. Such dedication across academia has been a joy to watch. Thank you for inspiring us.

Janie also specifically thanks her children, Chas and Samantha (Sam), for their patience as she worked at home when playtime was calling. She thanks Eric for his encouragement while writing "just one more chapter." Thank you to the Psychology Department of Georgia Southern University, an incredibly dedicated group of faculty members and supportive department chair, Dr. Michael Nielsen. Finally, much appreciation is given to the Society for the Teaching of Psychology for keeping the art and science of teaching alive and well.

Beth is thankful for the continued support and encouragement of her colleagues at Randolph College, in particular the faculty members in the Psychology Department. It is wonderful to be part of a department and an institution where the faculty is dedicated to teaching excellence, and both the faculty and administration understand the value of the scholarship of teaching and learning. Last, but not least, Beth thanks her incredible family: her husband, Doc, and daughters, Lauren and Meagan. They are all always understanding of the balancing act required between time "at home" and time "at work."

About the Authors

Janie H. Wilson received her PhD in experimental psychology from the University of South Carolina in 1994. Since that time, she has been teaching and conducting research at Georgia Southern University. In the classroom, Dr. Wilson specializes in teaching and learning in statistics and research methods and maintains a strong focus on involving undergraduates in her research as well as mentoring students to complete their own projects. For two decades, Dr. Wilson has taken students to conferences to present their research in the form of talks and posters, and she has published with undergraduates and graduate students as well.

Research interests include rapport in teaching based on empirical data on the first day of class, electronic communications, and interactions with students in a traditional classroom. A current project involves the development and validation of a professor-student rapport scale. Publications include a statistics textbook, *Essential Statistics*, with Pearson, as well as two upcoming texts with Sage. Dr. Wilson has contributed numerous chapters to edited books, including chapters in *The Evaluation of Teaching*; *The Teaching of Psychology: An Empirically Based Guide to Picking, Choosing, & Using Pedagogy*; *Effective College and University Teaching*; *Teaching Ethically: Challenges and Opportunities*; *Best Practices for Teaching Statistics and Research Methods in the Behavioral Sciences*; and *Empirical Research in Teaching and Learning: Contributions from Social Psychology*. She has coedited several books, including *Teaching Controversial Topics in Psychology*, *Best Practices for Technology-Enhanced Learning*, and a current project designed to help professors conduct and publish research in the scholarship of teaching and learning. Dr. Wilson has published in numerous journals, including *Teaching of Psychology*, *Journal of the Scholarship of Teaching and Learning*, *Journal of Classroom Interaction*, *College Teaching*, and *Assessment & Evaluation in Higher Education*. Finally, she has presented over 60 conference presentations, including several invited keynote addresses.

Dr. Wilson served as the American Psychological Association (APA) program chair for Division Two, the Society for the Teaching of Psychology (STP), as well as program director overseeing all programming efforts by STP. She currently serves as the vice president of programming for Division 2 of APA. She was honored with the College of Liberal Arts Award of Distinction in Teaching in 2003, the Georgia Southern University Award for Excellence in Contributions to Instruction in 2004–2005, the Georgia Southern University Scholarship of Teaching and Learning Award in 2012, and the Ruffin Cup award for excellence in contributions to the College of Liberal Arts and Social Sciences in 2013.

Beth M. Schwartz received her PhD in cognitive psychology from the State University of New York at Buffalo in 1991. Since that time, she has been on the faculty at Randolph College (formerly Randolph-Macon Woman's College) where she is currently the Thoresen Professor of Psychology, department chair, and assistant dean of the College. Dr. Schwartz's early work focused on factors that influence the accuracy of child witnesses, in particular how changes in the legal system can create a more age-appropriate interview for young children. Her current research program focuses on the scholarship of teaching and learning, examining pedagogical changes that can lead to more effective teaching and learning, and investigating the influence of honor systems on academic integrity.

In both programs of research, Dr. Schwartz focuses on providing undergraduate students with opportunities for research experience, involving students in her research program, as well as advising students interested in conducting their own investigations. As a result, many students have authored published work, presented at national conferences, and have obtained doctorate degrees. Dr. Schwartz has worked with over 1,000 students at Randolph College. She has presented 100 professional talks at conferences and is the author, co-author, and co-editor of over 20 books, book chapters, and professional articles in scholarly peer-reviewed journals. Her work has appeared in journals such as the *Journal of Higher Education, Law and Human Behavior, Ethics and Behavior,* and the *Journal of the Scholarship of Teaching and Learning.*

Dr. Schwartz was the founder of the Faculty Development Center at Randolph, serving as faculty development coordinator from 2000 to 2007 on her campus, providing faculty with programming focused on refining teaching to become most effective in the classroom. With these programs, she helped create an environment in which discussing the scholarship of teaching and learning is a norm. In her role as assistant dean of the College, she continues her involvement in SoTL on her own campus. She is coauthor of *An EasyGuide to APA Style* (2012, with Eric Landrum and Regan Gurung), *Optimizing Teaching and Learning: Catalyzing Pedagogical Research* (2009, with Regan Gurung), coeditor of *Evidenced-Based Teaching in Higher Education* (2012, with Regan Gurung), and coeditor of *Child Abuse: A Global View* (2001, with Michelle McCauley and Michele Epstein). She is a member of the American Psychological Association, a Fellow of the Society for the Teaching of

Psychology (Division 2 of APA), and a member of the Association for Psychological Science. In addition, she is currently involved in Division 2 of the American Psychological Association, recently serving as the first associate director for programming of regional conferences and currently serving as the vice president of recognitions and awards. At Randolph College, she teaches Introduction to Psychology, Cognitive Psychology, Research Methods, Forensic Psychology, and Sensation and Perception, and a Senior Research Capstone Course. Dr. Schwartz is an award-winning teacher, earning the 2001 Randolph College Gillie A. Larew Award for Outstanding Teaching as well as the 2006 Outstanding Teaching and Mentoring Award (from AP-LS); and most recently receiving the 2013 Randolph College Katherine Graves Davidson Award for Excellence in Scholarship.

SECTION I

Overview

Sharing the Wealth 1

Orientation to the Guide

Welcome! You opened this book to get help with professional presentations, and we hope to help. Your teacher can offer a lot of guidance too, but it is always nice to have an additional resource each step of the way as you prepare your presentations. You can use this book for step-by-step guidance on how to prepare a poster or an oral presentation but also for how you might overcome anxiety and how to connect with your audience. We have had the good fortune to work with many, many students over the years, so we have seen just about every situation that can come up. We offer helpful hints to avoid pitfalls and maximize success.

Although our examples in the text primarily focus on presenting empirical research, we regularly address the slight alterations needed for nonempirical work such as literature reviews. An additional issue is authorship. When you are the only author, you get to make all the decisions about when and where to present your work as well as the format. But you also take all on the responsibility! When you have a coauthor, you split the work and the credit. Either way, you should share your work with the scientific community. Below are several options in order of prestige:

1. Class presentation

2. Departmental presentation

3. On-campus miniconference

4. Regional, national, or international conference

5. Journal publication

First, let us address why you should present your work in the first place. Have you ever read a research article? Okay, we already know the answer to that question. It is highly unlikely that you would be ready to present your own work without first having read the work of other researchers. But let us give you the inside scoop on how a researcher gets to the point of having an article published for the world to see.

Just like you, each researcher begins with an idea. You know by now that you can get research ideas from going through your daily life, classroom discussions, reading books or articles, and chatting with other people about interesting issues related to behavior. That is exactly what published researchers did. Then they searched for journal articles related to the topic of interest and read, read, read to learn about what has already been studied. Researchers often take different approaches to a topic, studying it from different angles, but they also try to tie their study to others in some way. Sometimes this means using a survey that someone else used; sometimes it means sampling from a different population; sometimes the change involves bringing together two areas of research that have not yet been combined.

But as we said earlier, all research begins with an idea, and your idea must lead to sound methodology to test your hypotheses. As you probably know, the development of even a simple method quickly becomes complicated when you start looking at every tiny detail. And as a researcher, you *do* have to specify every detail (operationalize variables). After you lay out your method, you must get approval to run the study. Seeking approval requires submitting a proposal to an institutional review board (IRB) and often also includes completing some kind of training about how to treat participants in your research. Although ethics training and asking for approval from the IRB may seem like hoops to jump through, we hope you can see how important it is to make sure researchers are trained in ethics, and participants are protected from harm. Conducting research is a privilege that researchers consider almost sacred. Ethical treatment of participants even goes so far as to be on time for your studies and be kind, but these details must be covered in another book.

After researchers gain approval from the IRB, they can test participants and hope results come out to tell an interesting story that can be shared with the world. Does this always happen? You probably know that the answer is *no*. Often a researcher can run an entire study and find no significant results. Yes, it happens to all of us. Always try to keep in mind that we do not necessarily want significance; we want the truth. If the truth is that a specific independent variable (IV) does not cause an outcome we expected, we can either find other approaches to our question or learn that the IV did not affect the dependent variable (DV) after all.

Will nonsignificant results be published? Probably not. Failure to publish may seem unfair given that we were only seeking truth in the first place, but journal editors do not know if lack of significance means truly no relationship existed or if a researcher simply ran a sloppy study. Without certainty that a clean, well-organized study was conducted, publication is not possible, and we have to accept that an editor can never be sure.

Before we leave this part of the publication discussion, we should admit that even studies with significant results may not get published. A study must be well-written and have a meaningful message to share. Even then, authors realize that most reputable journals have high rejection rates. Details on how to write a good manuscript are beyond the scope of this book, but Chapter 14 offers step-by-step instructions on how to submit an article for publication.

For now, let us return to the issue of the journal article you read that *did* get published. After getting a research idea, reading published articles on the topic, devising a method, completing ethics training, gaining IRB approval, and getting a significant result (when analyzing the data using statistics software), the researcher wrote either a presentation or a manuscript. Often, a researcher will begin to share his or her work with a presentation (in either poster or talk format) to have a chance to speak with other researchers in person and get ideas about how to interpret the results or a potential next step in the research area.

Of course, if you read the journal article, the researcher also submitted a manuscript and published it. The publication process is an adventure unto itself, and we will take you through that process in Chapter 14. What we want you to take away from this discussion is that the published researcher goes through the exact same process you go through. The process is not magic and out of your reach; it just requires knowledge, motivation, and following a step-by-step process that leads to sharing your work with others. We provide that step-by-step process for you in this book.

Ultimately, research really does not mean a thing if it is not shared with the world. If you are reading this book, you have work to present. The biggest parts of your challenge are behind you, and it is time to celebrate your research by showing it to others. You have reached an exciting time in the research process, and you should be proud of your accomplishments. We know if you completed a research paper or project you have at least one of the following to share:

1. A literature review with no data collected

2. An empirical study with nonsignificant results

3. An empirical study with significant results

Any of these options works just fine. You can share what you have learned in either a poster or talk format. Even if you have a study with non-significant results, you can gain valuable experience with presentations.

Presenting your work to others moves you forward in your professional development, and you will be glad you did it!

In this *EasyGuide*, we offer the following:

- Overcoming fear of public speaking
- Choosing the method of presentation and making it happen (timelines)
- Details of creating and giving a poster presentation
- Details of creating and giving an oral presentation
- Professionalism and managing your audience
- How to best prepare yourself for presentations
- Assessing your presentation (getting feedback)
- Submitting your work for publication: the ultimate way to share your work

Throughout the *EasyGuide*, we refer to the most popular programs used to create elements of presentations, but you can use the programs you are most comfortable with. Specifically, we use

- SPSS for data analysis,
- Excel to create graphs,
- Word to make tables,
- PowerPoint 2010 to create posters and oral presentations,
- Prezi for oral presentations, and
- Keynote for Mac oral presentations.

You might be tempted to focus on the chapters covering poster or oral presentations, depending on what your needs are. We encourage you to read over other chapters too, because you would benefit from learning the best approach to mentally and physically preparing yourself for a presentation as well as learning how to read your audience and build a network of colleagues.

In this book, we have also chosen to include step-by-step instructions on how to submit your work for potential publication. Students rarely consider this option, perhaps because publication is such unexplored territory. We take away some of the mystery with example cover letters and detailed information about what to expect.

Finally, the Appendices offer valuable information that we hope you use. Take a look at the checklists for posters and talks in Appendix A to make sure you are well-prepared and avoid surprises. Consider asking your colleagues or teachers to assess your presentation using the sample rubrics in Appendix B. If you and your teacher agree that your work has a good chance of being published, read over Chapter 14 for numerous details of the process.

We hope our years of helping students present their research and taking students to conferences will benefit you. We are truly grateful for all that our students have taught us as they join our professional community of researchers. And we look forward to you joining the community as well.

Do Not Let Fear Stop You 2

Overcoming Anxiety

D oes the thought of public speaking terrify you? Maybe you are one of the lucky students who merely feels a few butterflies in the stomach. Either way, it is perfectly natural to feel some level of anxiety when planning to present in front of others. A little anxiety can actually be beneficial, prompting you to focus and prepare before you speak. But too much fear can be a problem. No worries, we will help you reduce your anxiety and perform at your best.

Fight or Flight . . . or Speech

Fear of evaluation stimulates all sorts of bodily responses that can get in the way of presentations. Our hearts beat a little faster, breathing becomes more rapid and shallow, saliva dries up, and sweat begins to form. Our bodies tell us that we are threatened in some way.

In fact, our bodies would react the same way to a large bear attacking, a knife-wielding mugger, or a postapocalyptic zombie attack. No matter what the threat, we feel pretty much the same. Let us begin with some logic right here. Standing in front of people and talking simply is *not* as bad as a bear, thief, or zombie. We need to put things in perspective and laugh at our own bodies for responding to public speaking as though a flesh-eating undead monster stands before us. Public speaking might feel highly threatening to you at first, but you will live through the experience, unlike the potential that exists with a zombie.

You might have noticed the use of *our* a lot in the previous paragraphs. That is because fear of public speaking is common to all people. We have been teaching for a long time and still feel anxious when we step in front of a new class. In fact, we admit that we have all the natural stress reactions for at least the first week of classes each term. Only after we get to know students a little does the anxiety begin to fade. Probably many (or all) of your teachers feel the same way.

You might be thinking that your case is special because you are an introvert. You enjoy time alone and are more of a private person who feels self-conscious around others. Maybe you think you already have a mark against you because you do not enjoy social interactions or being the center of attention as much as the extravert does. But introversion is not a problem; just keep in mind a few well-known introverts who managed to perform pretty well. You are in excellent company with the likes of Albert Einstein, Dwight D. Eisenhower, Susan B. Anthony, Audrey Hepburn, Tom Hanks, Meryl Streep, David Letterman, Barbara Walters, and J. K. Rowling, all of whom delivered successful public presentations. And you can too. Recognize that you might have to work a little harder to prepare yourself, and you might even need to do relaxation exercises (examples are below). Even if you have a full-blown social phobia, you can work through it with preparation, relaxation, and practice. Eventually you will learn that public speaking is doable and not nearly the threat you once thought it was.

Relaxation Exercises

By now you may have your own approaches to relaxing when you are stressed. As long as your approach does not include alcohol or other maladaptive activities, use the methods that work for you. Typical relaxation behaviors can include deep breathing, picturing yourself giving a good presentation, and even drinking water.

A quick internet search for "relaxation techniques" yields a wealth of information to reduce stress. Staff members at the Mayo Clinic (MayoClinic.com) point out that relaxation techniques generally are simple, free, and can be practiced just about anywhere. Although you already know that relaxing reduces stress (e.g., reduces blood pressure and heart rate), additional benefits include increased blood flow and better concentration. No matter how you look at it, relaxing is good for you, particularly when you relax using natural methods such as those outlined by the Mayo Clinic:

- Autogenic relaxation: practice self-induced concentration, perhaps on a calming visual scene, while relaxing muscles
- Progressive muscle relaxation: tense and release specific muscles or muscle groups, showing you the difference between tense and relaxed muscles

- Visualization: imagine a peaceful setting; employ as many senses as possible (e.g., imagine the smells and sounds in that setting)

In general, relaxation techniques have in common a focus on muscle awareness and relaxation, clearing the mind, and deep breathing. In fact, WebMD.com suggests a simple breathing exercise: Focus on your stomach, imagining the center of you as deep and peaceful. Breathe slowly and deeply, remaining focused on the movement of your stomach. With each long exhale, allow your body to relax and your chin to drop to your chest (if you are sitting). Through 10 inhale-exhale combinations, relax more with each exhale.

In addition to deep breathing, massage can help relax you, creating an awareness of your body and releasing muscle tension through touch. Although we recommend massage by someone else so you can focus on receiving touch, you might also try self-massage. Finally, stretching programs of exercise such as yoga can enhance awareness of your muscles and any tension found there.

If we move away from a focus on the body, we can consider certain rituals that may work for people. WebMD.com suggests being mindful, living in the moment. Being mindful involves paying attention to your surroundings and appreciating the beauty and peacefulness found there. For example, focus your mind on a leaf in front of you or the swirl patterns on your fingertips. As an alternative, you might drink green tea if that behavior tends to relax you. If you have never tried to relax with a cup of tea, you are in luck. You can begin an association between tea and relaxation by creating a peaceful environment while sipping a cup of tea. Over time, tea will become associated with relaxation, and you will have a new behavior to use whenever you want to return to that relaxed state. You might also try listening to music, but you probably should avoid acid rock or angry rap. When all else fails, you might interact with friends or a pet. Again, we do not suggest an angry or energetic interaction. Social support is important for relaxation as well as a general sense of well-being.

We have suggested various relaxation techniques to deal with any stress associated with public presentations; however, relaxing is a good skill to learn for life in general. With practice, you will get better at relaxing. In fact, increasing body awareness through training in relaxation techniques will teach you what tense muscles feel like. Over time, you should be able to recognize tense muscles as soon as you begin to respond to stress. You can train yourself to relax when you feel tense. We should offer one caution: Some people report that relaxing tension and calming mental chatter opens the mind to thoughts and emotions usually buried under daily stressors. Although the newly uncovered thoughts and emotions can be uplifting, insightful, or even offer an important epiphany, they also can be scary. As always, keep yourself mentally well by speaking to a health-care provider if you feel distress. Even uncomfortable insights can offer the chance for growth, as long as you have proper support and stay safe.

Sleep Hygiene

We know that sleep deprivation is not something new for most college students, with many students pulling all-nighters to meet paper deadlines or to study for an exam. In a state of sleep deprivation, our brain functioning is not at its peak. We may have difficulty thinking and remembering, stutter or have slurred speech, speak in a monotone voice, and have low levels of energy. With less sleep, you may reduce your ability to perform complex mental tasks. Specifically, a public presentation of your work is a mental task that requires clear thinking and focused concentration.

If you have trouble sleeping for a few days before your presentation, realize that your body will make up sleep as needed. Of course, you can always speak with your physician if lack of sleep is a hazard (e.g., when driving a car), but most of us have times when we cannot sleep, and we manage to perform adequately until sleep returns.

Some ways to encourage sleep, in no particular order, include the following:

- Avoid naps
- Drink warm milk
- Exercise in the evening (but not just before bedtime)
- Eat turkey
- Go to bed the same time each night and wake up at the same time regardless of sleep quality
- Avoid nonsleep activities in your bed (such as watching an exciting show)
- Turn out all lights
- Create a comfortable and quiet environment
- Read a boring book
- Avoid eating a heavy meal before bed or going to bed hungry
- Close your eyes and listen to your deep breathing
- If thoughts crowd your mind, make a note of what you will think about or do tomorrow; a note takes away the worry of forgetting an obligation

Try each of these approaches or one of your own, as long as your approach is quiet and useful. And if you are the type of person who can fall asleep but cannot stay asleep for long periods of time, you have two options:

- Get out of bed and do something useful; accomplish whatever is on your mind
- Close your eyes and concentrate on slow breathing; often you will fall asleep again

In the morning after a poor night's sleep, get up and tackle your day. Splash cold water in your face, take a tepid shower, and give some attention to your appearance. Even though you might feel tired, a positive outlook will help you address the day. We realize our advice sounds very 1950s, but it really does help to be positive after a poor night's sleep. After all, what is your alternative?

Final Cautions

When you arrive at your presentation, stress might be at the front of your awareness. Regardless, here is what *not* to do:

We do not suggest urgently reviewing your notes immediately before a presentation, especially if your presentation is a talk. Perhaps you will want to review your talk or poster the night before you present, but the day of the presentation, consider enjoying the conference, talking with colleagues, and attending other sessions. Particularly with a talk, you might be tempted to continually make changes to your slides; at some point you must leave your presentation alone! Making changes last minute is likely to just cause more stress rather than less. You will simply feel less prepared because of the lack of practice with the new changes.

When you are ready to give your talk, do not admit to the audience that you are afraid. Many students make this mistake because they think admitting fear will reduce it, and they hope their audience will go easy on them to be nice. Neither of these outcomes actually happens. When a student admits fear, it just becomes more salient for having spoken about it. And the audience feels uncomfortable. In fact, an audience should not expect less from a nervous student because being nervous does not excuse lack of preparation. A lenient audience does not do any favors for a speaker. So plan to work through your nervousness with solid overpreparation, and let your audience concentrate only on the information you give them in a winning, professional manner.

How Do I Get Started? 3

Some of you may be creating a presentation for a class, and your audience will be other students and your teacher. All of the advice in this book will help you. However, we hope that most of you eventually plan to present your work at a conference. To help you down that path, let us remove some of the mystery surrounding conferences.

Choosing a Conference

Conferences can range in scope from local to international. Local conferences include those at your school, where other students and perhaps teachers present their work on the campus or nearby. As you might imagine, local conferences are a great place to begin making presentations. Too often, people shun their own backyard opportunities in favor of leaving town. If you have access to a local conference, attend! You might also have access to a regional conference, where your state or a few states create a region of researchers and offer a conference. The benefit of a regional conference again is the convenience of staying fairly local, perhaps knowing others who are attending the conference, and saving money on hotels or at least travel costs if the conference is nearby. A national conference is defined as drawing researchers from across the United States. Even a national conference may end up being held near you, which is a nice bonus. Finally, an international conference could be held anywhere in the world (even in your own town) and draws people from many countries. As you may have guessed, presenting your work at a national or international conference is most impressive because you will have a more diverse audience, but at this stage in your career, you just need to focus on presenting *somewhere*.

One of the perks of choosing a larger conference geared toward professors is the big-name researchers who will attend and probably give presentations. In fact, a conference features keynote speakers, and hearing a keynote talk is a conference highlight. You might be surprised to see that a keynote speaker is someone you read about in your textbook or someone you referenced in your paper. The author might even have devised a key term in your area of interest or moved the field forward a great deal. And you get to hear him or her speak.

On a related note, well-published researchers will visit poster sessions as well as oral presentations and talk with people who present their work. We both vividly recall a famous author stopping by a poster to chat at a conference early in our careers. What a rush! We imagine it feels like meeting your favorite actor, musician, or politician. Yes, we even made geeky jokes about not washing the hand that we shook.

To be fair, many well-known authors will give keynote talks (*addresses*) at smaller conferences. But overall, the larger the conference scope (e.g., national or international), the more likely you will see, hear, and meet authors you admire.

After you or your teacher have identified a conference, check the conference website to find out if organizers invite submissions. Keep in mind that some conferences only offer invited programming and do not allow researchers to submit their work for possible inclusion in the conference. If the conference does allow outside submissions, find out if you have the option of a poster or paper (also called a *talk*) presentation. Later in this chapter, we discuss what each type of presentation requires from you.

Each conference has a target audience, which means they also have a target for presenters. Most likely, a national or international conference focuses on professors as their presenters and audience. Keep in mind that you could consider coauthoring your presentation with a faculty member. Because your instructor likely did help you with the research, this works well. You and your instructor can decide order of authorship, who will attend the conference (you alone or both you and your teacher), and who will present the work. That said, many conferences are moving toward student-friendly sessions to welcome and encourage the next generation of researchers (students currently in their undergraduate or graduate career). Find out if the conference encourages student submissions, or better yet, ask your professor or mentor. Usually if student submissions are welcome, the conference flyer or website will say so. If you are an undergraduate, know that several annual conferences focus entirely (or almost entirely) on undergraduate research. We strongly encourage you to present at an undergraduate conference before moving on to a more diverse audience. Organizers of undergraduate conferences usually make sure students feel welcomed and encouraged. If you are a graduate student, you should be welcome at any conference beyond the undergraduate level, particularly if your mentor is a coauthor.

Next, obtain instructions on how to submit a proposal. Most conferences have a website that includes details on these instructions. Conference organizers generally require a cover page and an abstract that summarizes your work. Some conferences also require that you register for the conference and pay when you submit your abstract for review. They do this to make sure you will present your work if they accept it. Even if they do not require registration and payment at the time of submission, you are required to present if accepted. You may find this expectation written on the cover page you submit or on the website. Either way, know that it is highly unprofessional to submit an abstract without a 100% commitment to attend the conference and present your work.

Let us take a minute to talk about your submission. Most conferences include a submission process that includes evaluation of your proposed presentation. That evaluation will then determine if your submission is accepted for presentation at the conference. So you need to make your submission competitive. It goes without saying (but we will say it anyway) that you need to write coherently and avoid typos. You should also focus on active voice and avoid passive voice whenever possible. Although APA style does not emphasize references in an abstract (because they will occur later in the paper anyway), it is perfectly acceptable to include references and a brief APA-style reference section in your abstract submission. In fact, we have even appended a graph to depict a main result in our submissions, just to give conference organizers a better feel for what we would present, if accepted. We are not suggesting that you overwhelm organizers by sending a long abstract; one single-spaced page is plenty, and half a page is fine too as long as you cover the information. Check for word limits the conference organizers might set, and do not go over the limit. A general rule of thumb is two sentences to summarize each main section of a paper: Introduction, Method, Results, and Discussion. You end up with an eight-sentence abstract with a few key references and a reference list at the bottom of the abstract. Sure, you can deviate from this formula, but the approach works well when you need a place to begin.

Many conferences—particularly those that cater to student researchers—will ask your professor to serve as a mentor and sign off on the cover page that he or she approves of the submission. Even if the form does not require a teacher mentor, it is always a good idea to get feedback from someone who knows about research presentations.

As one final conference note, when proposals have been accepted and a program is complete, most organizers will post details on a website. You might want to check the final program to see your name there. A complete program, likely with even more detail, will be available at the conference, so remember to go the registration desk when you get to the conference. You can pick up your program and name badge. Larger conferences may also offer a small gift such as a bag or backpack. Be sure to keep your program after the conference ends so you can have evidence that you attended and presented. And you can show your mom, dad, grandmother, or children how impressive you are. On that same note of evidence, be sure to save all receipts if you will be reimbursed by your school. Most institutions will not reimburse any expense without a receipt.

Poster or Oral Presentation?

Usually you will be able to choose whether to present your research in poster or oral format. After identifying a conference that you can attend and getting an okay from your teacher, the next step is to let the conference know whether you would like to present a poster or an oral presentation. This decision needs to happen when you submit your work to a conference. Conference organizers can only accept a certain number of posters and papers given the time frame and space available for the conference. In general, it is easier to get a poster accepted than an oral presentation. The conference cover page usually asks you to indicate which type of presentation you prefer.

We suggest that students present in a poster format first because it is a bit less stressful and provides more interaction with the audience; however, your professor might encourage an oral presentation, or the conference may only accept oral presentations. If you get to choose, we still encourage a poster first. In this chapter, we provide an overview of the two kinds of presentations to help you decide which one you want to do. Later chapters provide many details on how to accomplish each type of presentation.

Poster Presentations

A poster presentation involves summarizing the material you want to present. Your summary will be visual and usually includes sections that match up with an APA-style manuscript (e.g., introduction, method). Your instructor might be willing to help you get started and might even have an example poster or digital template to share with you. With a poster, preparation is the biggest part of a smooth conference experience. Work hard (and early) to create a close-to-perfect poster, and you can look forward to displaying your research in a fairly low-stress setting. At the conference, you will pin up your poster and refer to it as a visual aid while you chat with people who stop by.

During a poster session, you generally will present your poster in a session where many other researchers present their posters as well. The room likely will have several bulletin boards in it, and you will use pushpins to secure the poster to the board.

Then you will stand near your poster (and others presenters stand by theirs) for 1 to 2 hours and answer any questions from conference attendees who visit your poster. Think of a poster session as a drop-in function. People come and go in a fairly casual manner, and you talk with them about your research. Although we will provide much more detail on how to create a poster and discuss it (see Chapters 4 and 5), this summary should indicate how low stress a poster presentation can be.

Poster Timeline and Tasks

If you decide to submit a poster proposal, your research should be complete. In other words, researchers should not submit a conference proposal based on what they hope to accomplish; submit finished research. After submitting a proposal of completed research, follow the table below to prepare for your poster presentation.

We realize that if you are presenting a poster at the end of a term, you will not necessarily have long periods of time to prepare. Often students are asked to give a presentation based on recent work. That is just the nature of the academic year. It takes time to put together a literature review or conduct an experiment, and you likely used most of your term to accomplish the research project. In the table below, we present the best-case scenario to prepare your poster. If you do not have time to prepare months in advance, change *months* to *weeks*, and change *weeks* to *days* in the table. The main message here is to avoid procrastination and address the steps outlined in the table. Preparing your presentation in advance is particularly important if you are interested in getting feedback from your instructor. It is not fair to ask your professor to review your work within a day or two. Give your teacher as much time as possible to provide valuable feedback. If you wait too long, you will be asking for feedback that you do not have time to use in your presentation. The last thing you want to do is get feedback and ignore it. We have seen that happen, and it is not a good situation.

Table 3.1 Time Table for a Long-Term Research Project: Poster	
Time Before Poster Presentation	**Task**
3–6 months	Conduct your empirical research or literature review.
3–6 months	Write your manuscript, including an abstract.
3–6 months	With the help of your instructor, identify a conference and submit an abstract of your work for consideration. If your poster presentation is in class, move to the next step.
2–3 months	Create a first draft of your poster, and ask your teacher for input.
1–2 months	Choose the format of your poster. Be sure to use a font large enough to read from a distance. Carefully proofread your poster multiple times.

(Continued)

Table 3.1 (Continued)

Time Before Poster Presentation	Task
1–2 months	Discuss your poster with a few people who are unfamiliar with your topic. Make changes to clarify as needed.
2–3 weeks (procrastinating can cause a problem when the copy shop has a broken printer or several jobs ahead of you)	Take a digital file of your poster to a copy shop. Be sure of the correct size. Decide if you want to print in full color, which might be pricey.
1–2 weeks	Read over your poster in the larger size. If you locate an embarrassing mistake, rush back to the copy shop.
1–2 weeks	Make one-page copies of your poster for handouts. Usually 25 copies is a good number. Be sure to include your name and contact information.
1 week	Practice what you will say when people stand in front of your poster. Be able to summarize the project within a few minutes.
1 week	Put everything away neatly and relax!

Oral Presentations

A paper presentation requires a summary of your paper in PowerPoint format. One good alternative to PowerPoint is Prezi, and Keynote is available to Mac users. We cover how to use each program later in the book. A talk is brief; you usually only get 15 minutes. In those 15 minutes you have to present your entire paper or study, which means you have to make those minutes count. If your study involves a method and your own results, audience members do not want to hear a great deal about your literature review. They want to learn about your personal addition to the literature.

Spend a few minutes setting the stage with your literature review. What are you studying? What is already known on the topic? In other words, use your introductory slides to bring attendees up to speed on your topic. Quickly. Briefly. Then give a good deal of detail on your own method. What was your independent variable (IV), if you had one? What are your outcome measures? You might even want to provide a handout that summarizes the measures you used and offers references to locate them. Again, be brief in a handout. A handout should only be a page or two. Next offer your results in detail, but rely on figures if possible. People love pictures! The next section is the discussion, and it should merely put your results into the context of the larger literature. Briefly indicate how your study extended knowledge of the topic. End with a list of key references, thank people you worked with on the project (especially your instructor), and thank the audience.

If you have a minute or two left at the end of your talk (and you should), you can ask the audience for questions, or the moderator of the session may do that for you. We will talk about handling questions in Chapter 11. You will find details on preparing an oral presentation in Chapters 6, 7, 8, and 9.

Oral Presentation Timeline and Tasks

Below we offer a timeline for tasks to accomplish and when to complete them. Some tasks will be similar to poster preparation, but take a look to make sure you get everything done on time. Although we offer the best-case scenario with a wealth of time to work, adjust times as needed for a single-term project. Just as in the poster timeline, we suggest changing *months* to *weeks* and *weeks* to *days* if you are working within one term.

Table 3.2 Time Table for a Long-Term Research Project: Oral Presentation

Time Before Oral Presentation	Task
3–6 months	Conduct your empirical research or literature review.
3–6 months	Write your manuscript, including an abstract.
3–6 months	With the help of your instructor, identify a conference and submit an abstract of your work for consideration. If your oral presentation is in class, move to the next step.
2–3 months	Create a first draft of your oral presentation, and ask your teacher for input.
1–2 months	Practice your talk in your head, then aloud, then to a friend, then to your teacher, making changes as needed each time.
1–2 weeks	Read over your presentation again; make small changes as needed.

(Continued)

Table 3.2 (Continued)

Time Before Oral Presentation	Task
1–2 weeks	Make copies of handouts (about 25). Handouts might include your abstract or an important table, graph, or survey (as examples). Be sure to include your name and contact information.
1 week	Make a clean hardcopy of your presentation to take with you. Write notes on the hardcopy if you would like.
1 week	Put everything away neatly and relax!

Now you know how to choose a conference, submit your work for possible inclusion, and consider a timeline to prepare a poster or oral presentation. You are ready to learn many details about building a poster, creating visual aids for oral presentations, considering behavioral choices before, during, and after your presentation, and even thinking about steps toward publishing your research!

SECTION II

Poster Presentations

Posters Are Not Just for Dorm-Room Walls 4

Now that you have chosen to present a poster, you are ready to learn how to create one. A poster is a visual display that summarizes your work and relies on APA-style paper sections to organize the research. If your study was an empirical one (either an experimental or correlational design), you know the main sections are introduction, method, results, and discussion. Sure, you also have an abstract, references, and probably figures or tables. You might even have an appendix. All of these sections are fine, but the main four will help guide your organization. Generally the paper summary is digitally pasted onto a single PowerPoint slide that is printed in a large format. Obviously this will mean deleting a great deal of what is in your paper so that your main points are displayed on the poster. Many conferences require a 3×4 foot poster, but you will need to check with the conference coordinator (or your instructor) to be sure of the correct dimensions.

Presenters sometimes have used alternate formats, including pasting white sheets onto colored poster board with about a 1-inch margin on all sides. Imagine several summary sheets, each framed by colored poster board. The effect was attractive, but at this point technology has moved us beyond such an approach.

We have also seen poster presentations where summary sheets are merely tacked to a board, and no framing or display is offered. As bad as this display looks, it is not as bad as when a presenter summarizes nothing and only prints a paper (perhaps in 12-point font), secures it to a board, and calls it a poster. Our goal in this section of the *EasyGuide* is to make sure you have a highly professional poster to share with the scientific community. In our opinion, the best format is a PowerPoint slide printed in the dimensions required by the conference or your instructor.

Poster Content

The poster format depends on the type of paper you are summarizing. An empirical study relies on APA-paper sections, which gives you clear guidance. If instead you conducted a literature review for your paper, the organization is a bit less obvious. We suggest following the organization of your paper, summarizing the main sections. For example, if you reviewed the literature on student attitudes toward instructors based on the way they look, you might use the following sections:

- A brief overview of what you are interested in
- A summary of literature on instructor attractiveness
- A review of the literature on style of dress while lecturing
- A summary of how instructor gender might influence results of the two variables above (especially given that gender is part of the way we look)
- Any research on instructor age as a variable tied to the way teachers look
- A take-home message given all that you learned while pulling together these related areas of research

You might also recreate a key effect or two from studies you found most relevant and interesting. By recreating, we mean putting together figures or tables based on results reported by the authors. Although you should not copy and paste an existing figure or table from a publication, you can create a graph of an effect based on numbers reported in a results section (for example). You can also retype a scale used to assess student ratings of the instructor, if a scale in a publication seemed particularly relevant. Just remember to cite the original source of the scale on your poster. As a final example, you can even add a picture or two of the way a professor with high evaluations might look, based on your research. Make sure you have the person's permission before displaying the picture. You get the idea. The poster is a lot more inviting with something other than just words. Make it pretty and welcoming with relevant visual features.

Creating a Poster: Step-by-Step Instructions

Before we begin our discussion of how to create a poster in PowerPoint, let us assure you that other software programs can be used to create posters, and even within PowerPoint, you have many options for how to approach the task. We will show you one way to get you started. Feel free to play with whatever software you choose. Create one slide with all of your information on it, then have it printed in the size you need. Remember, the conference or your teacher will specify the correct size.

Layout

In PowerPoint, a title slide will be chosen for you as a default beginning. We will make it a blank slide by clicking the Home tab at the top, then Layout next to New Slide. When the drop-down menu offers you different types of slide formats, click on Blank.

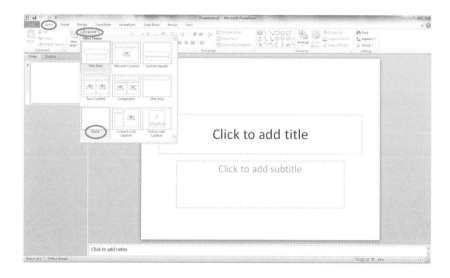

Now you have a blank slide, and you are ready to create a beautiful poster.

Our goal is to put pieces together that summarize an empirical study or literature review. With an empirical study, the poster will have several parts, including a title, abstract, introduction (literature review), method, results, discussion, references, and perhaps a figure, table, or appendix. As an example, look at the following layout for an empirical study. The two white boxes on the right can be used for graphs or other supporting materials that enhance visual interest. You might notice the extra pop we have added with pictures at the top and fading color across the background; these are options you can play with after you have learned the basics in this chapter. It is customary to include your school's logo on your poster, usually on the top panel. If you decide to use colors on your poster, stick with only two to three darker colors against a white (or light) background.

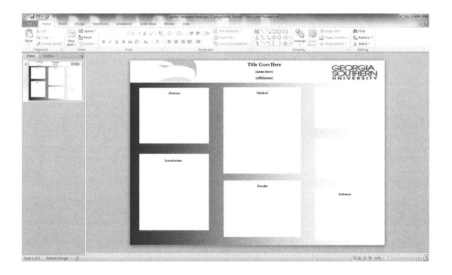

Notice that the information on the poster flows from top to bottom, then left to right. The direction of information follows a predictable pattern for Western readers. You might also seek symmetry, with boxes on the left and right. In Chapter 5, we explain how to add material such as pictures to your poster, and some people suggest that even graphic elements should be symmetrical, avoiding picture overload on only one side of your poster. We will leave that part to you; just remember that we are trying to draw people to a visually pleasant poster.

Now that you have an idea of our goal, we can talk about how to create a poster. After we have a template such as the slide above, we will add text boxes for words in each section. For a graph, we will simply create one in Excel and copy and paste the graph onto the poster, moving it to where we want it and resizing to fit our needs.

Text Boxes

First we need to create the title box across the top of the poster. We click the Insert tab at the top left of the computer screen. About halfway across the top, you will see a button marked Text Box. Clicking this option will turn your cursor into a T-shape.

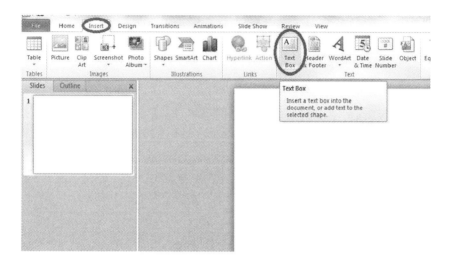

Move the T-shape to the upper left corner of the slide, hold down the left side of the mouse, and drag the T-shape to the right side and down a bit to create a box. When the mouse is released, a cursor will remain in the box, waiting for further instructions.

Before we type words, remember that we are merely formatting the slide to be ready for content later. Right click inside the text box. A box will open, and you should choose Format Shape from the bottom of the menu.

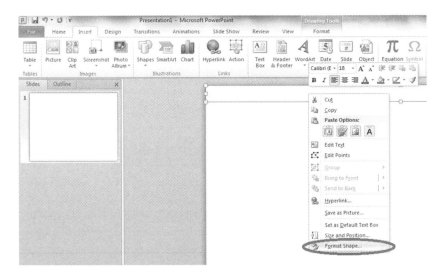

In the box that opens, click Text Box from the bottom left of the list.

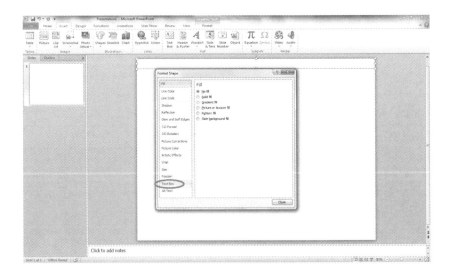

In the next box that opens, change Vertical alignment from Top to Middle. And under Autofit, select the circle next to Shrink text on overflow.

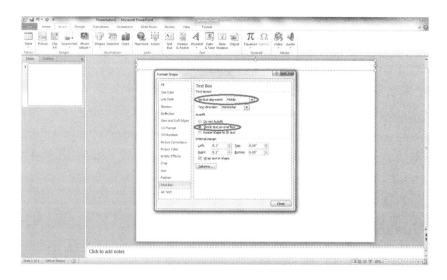

Click the Close button. You now will be able to finish formatting the box and know that whatever you later type in the box will be adjusted automatically to fit inside.

Next right click inside the title box again, choose Format Shape again, and click Line Color on the left. Choose Solid line by clicking the circle next to it, then change the line color to black.

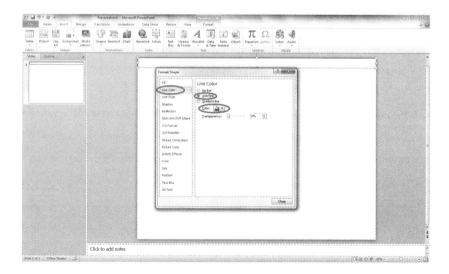

Close and return a third time to Format Shape. Under the options, this time click Line Style. Beside Width, change the font to 2 point, then Close. At this point you might have noticed that you can keep the Format Shape box open and make all of the changes we have discussed before clicking the Close button. We wanted to introduce pieces slowly so you could see each step.

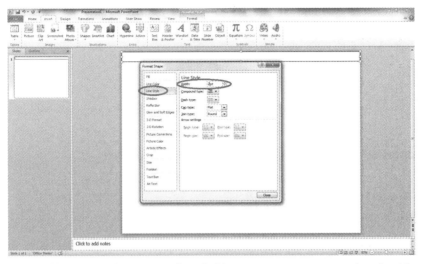

Finally, because later you will probably want your text centered in the title box, go ahead and right click inside the box once more. In the small box that opens on the top, click the center-text icon as shown below. (You can play with the style, color, and other features of your text box whenever you feel like being creative—but do not get too radical.)

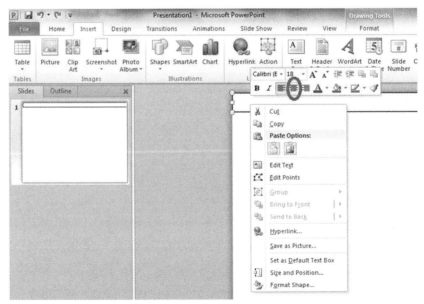

We can return to the title box later and enter text, or we can type right now. We will go ahead and show you what the text will look like using one of our posters.

Left click inside the title box and type. At first the words will get smaller with more lines because you set up the text to not overflow the box, but that is not a problem. After you have typed in the information, simply put your cursor (mouse) over the bottom small square on the text box, left click, and drag the box down to make it as large as you would like. We have also chosen to make the title text bold.

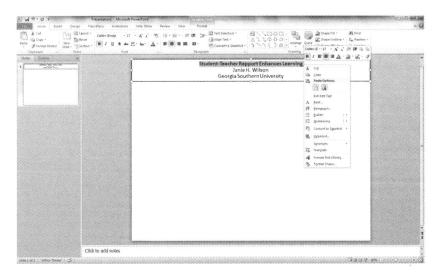

To add other boxes across your poster, follow the same procedure, but do not center the text. Left-side alignment for the remaining boxes will work well.

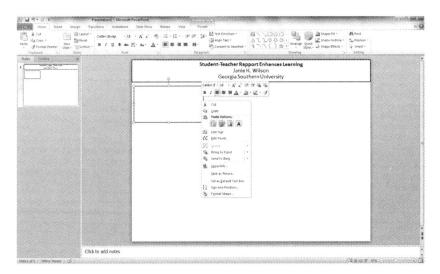

To make your life easier, the remaining boxes can be copied from this new one. Right click on the box, choose Copy, and then right click elsewhere on the slide to Paste the box. Repeat the Paste command as many times as you would like. Move and resize boxes until you like the number, locations, and sizes. You will notice that PowerPoint helps you align your boxes with dotted horizontal and vertical lines that appear as you are moving the boxes. You do not have to follow the lines, but it is a nice feature.

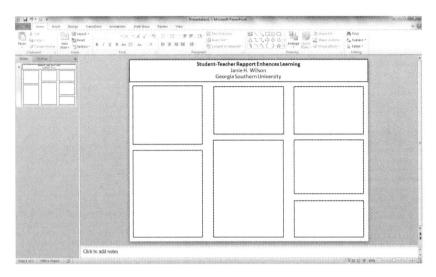

In the next screen capture, we show you that we have clicked into the first box under the title and entered text for our abstract as well as a heading to label the abstract.

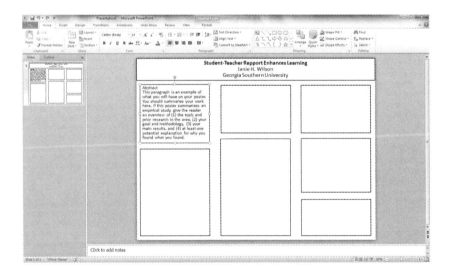

Double left click on top of the heading (Abstract), and in the top box that opens, click the centering icon and the bolding icon. Leave the text of the abstract aligned with the left side of the box, and make sure the abstract is readable from a distance of about 3 feet away. In fact, everything on your poster (with the possible exceptions of tables, appendices, and references) should be readable from 2 to 3 feet away, but it is particularly important that the abstract is readable so people can easily get an idea of your message.

Additional advice we can offer to increase readability is to keep the poster as simple as possible while also making it look interesting. Do not be afraid to have some white space rather than overwhelm every inch of your poster. Consider keeping your sentences simple and straightforward, while still conveying your message.

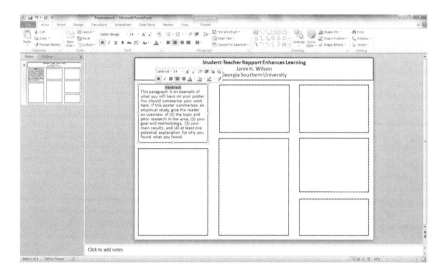

When you have completed all text, print it on one page by asking PowerPoint to Scale to Fit Paper when you are in the Print options.

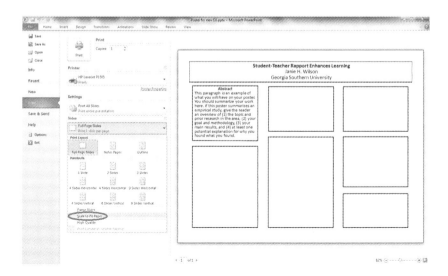

After printing a draft on regular-sized paper, read over your poster to look for errors. Yes, the print will be small, but you should be able to read it. If not, other people probably will not be able to read it from 2 to 3 feet away when you print the final poster on larger paper.

If you see no errors, we are amazed! When you *do* find errors and fix them, we suggest taking the digital file to a copy shop and asking them to print in the dimensions you need. Check on price first, and if you cannot afford a higher price, you might want to avoid printing in full color if you have chosen to add color in the PowerPoint file. The copy shop can usually print in grey for a lower cost than color. Even in grey, you can be proud of a well-formatted poster. After the poster is copied and ready to go, roll it loosely to avoid creases. And pat yourself on the back for creating, from start to finish, your first poster.

Adding Pizzazz to Posters 5

A poster should not be boring. One way to avoid being boring is to add interesting visual details that also enhance understanding of your message. The most common way to add interesting details beyond paragraphs of text is to include a figure or a table. Figures usually come in the form of a graph of your data. Graphs are so popular that readers have come to expect them, both in presentations and in manuscripts. In the next section, we offer detailed, step-by-step instructions on how to create a graph. We rely on graphing in Excel because it is the most widely used graphing software, but our description of what to include should guide you no matter which software package you choose.

Creating Graphs for Visual Interest

In order to graph data, you must first have data. If you ran an empirical study with quantitative data, you have some numbers to compile in a meaningful way. Keep in mind that graphs work best when the outcome variables (such as dependent variables, DVs) are interval or ratio data so they have math properties. You analyzed your data and hopefully collected descriptive information on your variables. For step-by-step details on how to analyze data from many designs, see *An EasyGuide to Research Design & SPSS* (Schwartz, B. M., Wilson, J. H., & Goff, D. M., 2015. Thousand Oaks, CA: Sage). Let us go through an example of how to use descriptive statistics to create a graph. If you ran an experiment that involved asking some people to drink caffeinated coffee and others to drink decaffeinated coffee, you might want to look at their heart rate after the drinks are consumed. The main question likely would be *Do people who drink caffeinated coffee have faster heart rates than those who drink coffee with no caffeine?*

Your data analysis showed you if the two groups differed, and if you asked for descriptive statistics, you can easily prepare a graph of your data. In a study such as this one, you would need to report the two averages (means) for the groups and a measure of variability within each group. The most straightforward measure of variability is standard deviation (SD), and you might recall that SD tells how scores are spread out within each group. Even though you want scores (means) to differ *between* the two groups, you do not want a lot of variability *within* a group. After all, everyone in the caffeine group drank caffeine; they were treated the same. You do not want a lot of variability among people who were all treated in the same way. Of course the same logic holds true for the decaffeinated-coffee condition. The point here is that people do not want to see just a graph with group means (in this case, a bar graph with two bars); they want you to indicate how much the values in each group were spread out. You need to graph the means and error bars, or SD. Some people call these T-bars because they look like little *T*s.

Any data-analysis software allows you to click a couple of options after entering your data to get descriptive statistics for your groups. Before we go any further, we can look at fictional data. Heart rate (the DV) is beats per minute in the columns.

Decaf coffee	Caffeine in coffee
70	89
65	76
50	73
78	69
92	95
58	102
86	113
59	81
79	88

Entering the data into SPSS (a popular statistics package) and asking for descriptive statistics gives us the following output.

Descriptive Statistics					
	N	Minimum	Maximum	Mean	Std. Deviation
Decaf	9	50.00	92.00	70.7778	14.00694
Caffeine	9	69.00	113.00	87.3333	14.34399
Valid N (listwise)	9				

Notice that we now know the average heart rate for people in each condition. We also have a number (the SD) for how those values are spread out *within* a group. Remember that we hope the SD is not a very high number.

It is time for us to take these descriptive data and create a graph. You can use the graph on your poster or in your oral presentation, and you really should consider adding a graph to your paper as well. In the next sections, we explain ways to graph a few types of data using different figures. We rely on Excel because it is widely available, but the basic ideas are the same regardless of the graphing software you choose.

Graphing a Nominal or Ordinal Independent Variable

The example above (coffee) used a nominal independent variable (IV). The two IV conditions, caffeinated coffee and decaffeinated coffee, merely represented two categories. (Note that an IV is manipulated; if you have a nonmanipulated variable, simply call it a pseudo-IV and continue with your analysis.) The outcome, or DV in the caffeine example, was heart rate, which is a ratio variable; a DV with math properties is crucial for the graph we are creating.

Because we already know the descriptive statistics for the caffeine example, we will write them below.

Decaf coffee	Caffeine in coffee
Mean (*M*) = 70.78	Mean (*M*) = 87.33
Standard Deviation (*SD*) = 14.01	Standard Deviation (*SD*) = 14.34

To graph in Excel, you can type in headings for the A1 and B1 positions and type the correct mean below each heading (A2 and B2 boxes). Do not let it bother you that some of the word is hidden; it will show up when you create a graph.

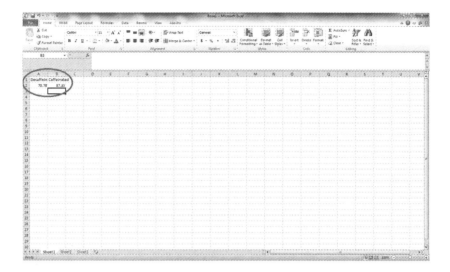

Next click the Insert Tab at the top, then click Column from the pictures of bar graphs that come up.

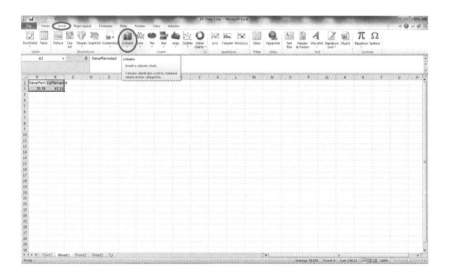

Choose the first option on the left, which is 2-D Column.

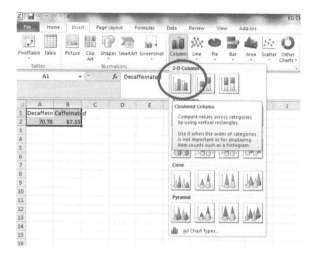

When you click it, a graph will appear in the middle of the spreadsheet.

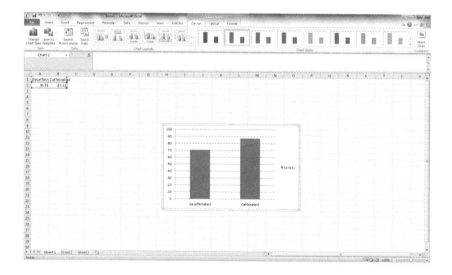

We do not want a graph stuck here in the page. We need to have it as a separate page. To do this, right click on the graph, then click Move Chart.

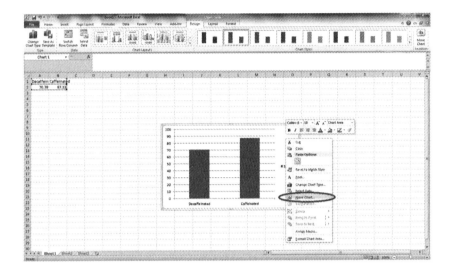

When you click on Move Chart, a new box will allow you to make the graph its own page.

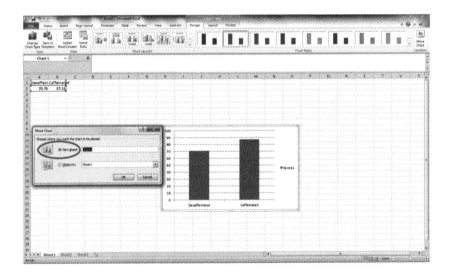

Select New sheet, then click OK for a larger graph on a separate page. This is the graph we will format for a presentation or manuscript.

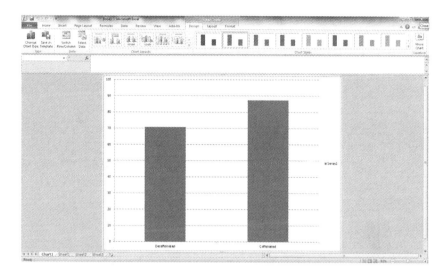

When formatting this graph, we will make it simpler and more reader-friendly. You can do the following edits in any order, of course, but we will start with removing the horizontal lines across the graph. Right click on one of the lines, then click Delete.

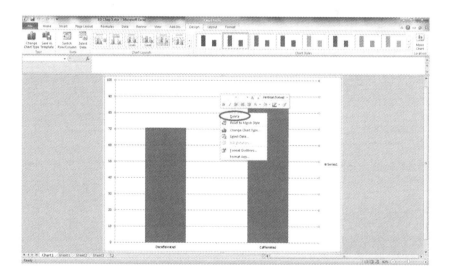

We also want to remove Series1 on the right side of the graph. Follow the same procedure to delete.

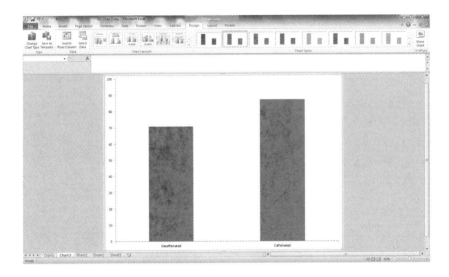

Next we will work on removing the blue color (fill) from the two bars. Right click inside one of the bars. On the box that opens, click Format Data Series.

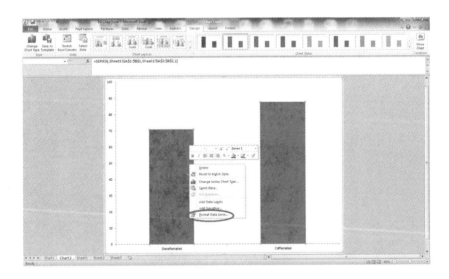

A new box will open (see on next page).

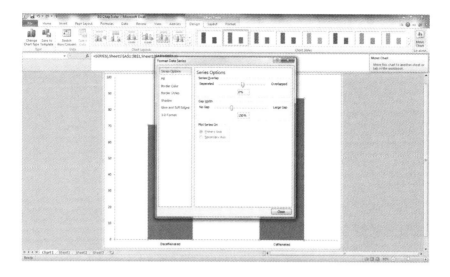

On the left side of the box, click Fill. In the box that opens, choose No Fill.

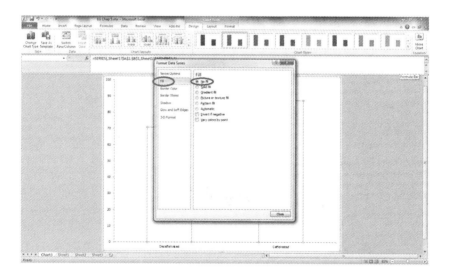

Again on the left side of the box, click Border Color, then Solid line, and change the color from blue to black.

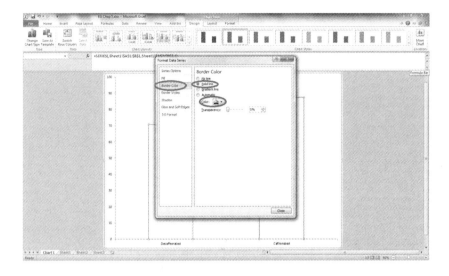

Click Close. Now we will enlarge the font sizes of numbers on the *Y*-axis and the two words on the *X*-axis. You might like them the way they are, but we prefer the font size to be about 16. Right click on any *Y*-axis number. In the top box that opens, change the font size from 10 to 16.

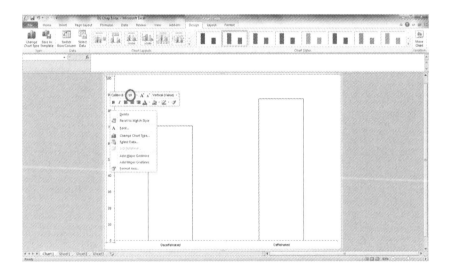

The font size of your *Y*-axis numbers will be more readable.

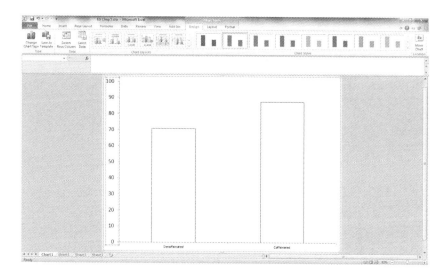

We will follow the same procedure to enlarge the two words on the X-axis.

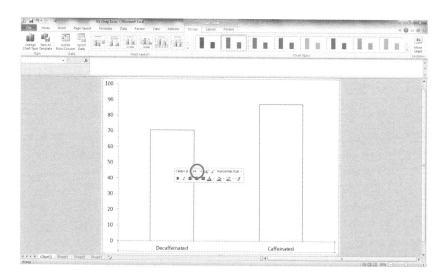

We are ready to label our axes. The X-axis title needs to indicate that the two groups are types of coffee, and the Y-axis needs to tell the reader that the data presented here are mean heart rates for the two groups. Still using the Chart Tools under the Layout tab at the top of the screen, look for Axis Titles. After you click that image, choose Primary Horizontal Axis Title then Title Below Axis.

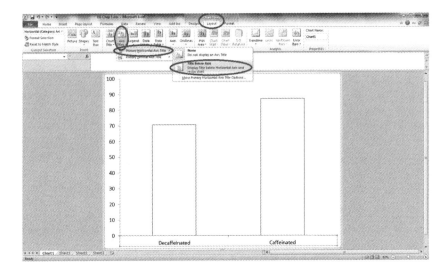

The cursor will be in an open box at the top of the screen. Enter "Type of Coffee" in the space, and click the Enter key on your keyboard to make it appear on the graph. Right click on the words, and change the font size to 16.

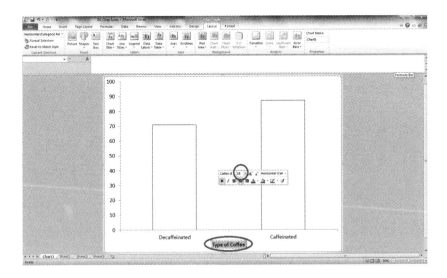

Follow a similar procedure for the *Y*-axis. Click Axis Titles, Primary Vertical Axis Title, and Rotated Title.

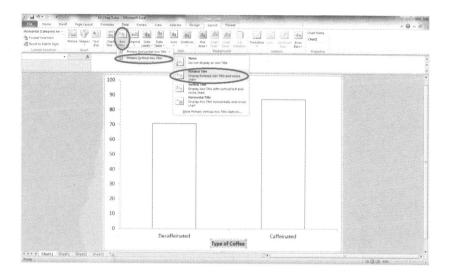

Type in Mean Heart Rate, Enter, highlight, right click, and change font to 16.

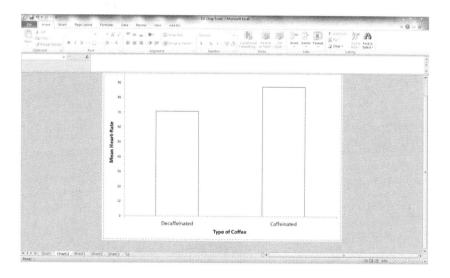

Finally, we need to make sure our graph includes SD to show the reader how much spread we had within a group. In other words, we need to show how much variability we had in heart rate within each condition. We simply look at our SPSS output for SD. For the group who drank decaffeinated coffee, $SD = 14.01$; for those who drank caffeinated coffee, $SD = 14.34$. Under Chart Tools and Layout tabs, click Error Bars, then More Error Bar Options.

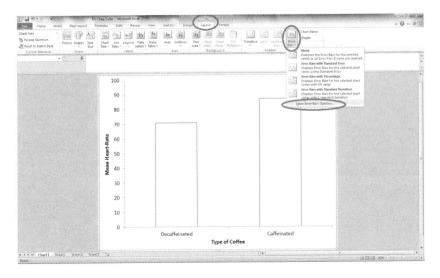

In the box that opens, under Error Amount, click Custom.

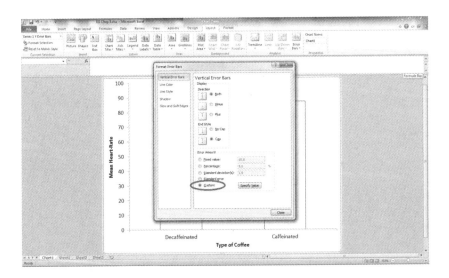

Next click Specify Value. In the top part of the box that opens, remove what is there and type "14.01,14.34" instead. This tells Excel that the SD for group 1 is 14.01, and SD should have an error bar that goes up from the top of the first column (bar) 14.01 units based on the Y-axis scaling. SD for the second group is 14.34, so the second bar should have a T-bar that goes up 14.34 units based on the Y-axis. Follow the same procedure to enter "14.01,14.34" in the opening just below the one you filled. This second box puts the same length error bars going downward. This might seem confusing, but take a look.

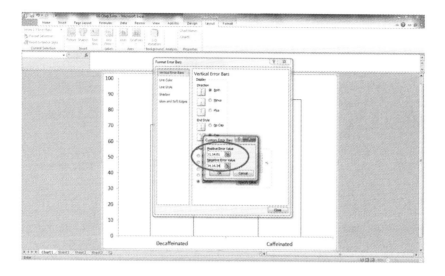

Click OK, then Close to see a lovely graph.

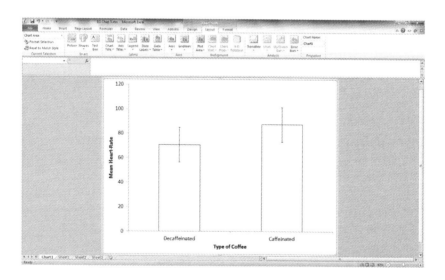

You probably recall from your statistics course that we report means (when designs allow means, such as this one), and we report one SD above and below the mean to let the reader know where most of the values in a specific group are located. By adding error bars (*SD*) to our graph, we show the reader plus-or-minus one *SD* for each group. In other words, we show where most of the values fall for each group. Larger error bars mean a lot of variability, which of course we do not want within a group where all people were treated the same.

Graphing an Interval or
Ratio Independent Variable

So far we have covered how to create a bar graph. A bar graph means your IV (or nonmanipulated pseudo-IV) is nominal or ordinal data. Separate categories, separate bars. And of course your DV is interval or ratio data. Otherwise, you could not even calculate a mean and standard deviation. Again, for a discussion of these design and analysis questions see *An EasyGuide to Research Design & SPSS* (Schwartz, B. M., Wilson, J. H., & Goff, D. M., 2015. Thousand Oaks, CA: Sage). Now we will move on to an IV of interval or ratio data. We cannot use separate bars for this graph because interval and ratio data represent values with math properties. In other words, you know that interval and ratio data do not have separate categories for levels. Instead we will use a line graph to indicate the continuity between numbers on interval and ratio variables.

As an example, imagine we wanted to examine ratings of relationship satisfaction across three durations: 30 days, 60 days, and 90 days. We might operationally define relationship satisfaction as a scale from 1 to 5, with higher numbers indicating a greater satisfaction. Further imagine we obtained the following data.

30 days	60 days	90 days
3	2	5
2	3	4
4	3	4
4	4	4
3	2	4
4	2	5
2	1	5
3	3	4
5	2	5

Below are descriptive statistics (means and standard deviations) for our three conditions.

Descriptive Statistics					
	N	Minimum	Maximum	Mean	Std. Deviation
Thirty	9	2.00	5.00	3.3333	1.00000
Sixty	9	1.00	4.00	2.4444	.88192
Ninety	9	4.00	5.00	4.4444	.52705
Valid N (listwise)	9				

As in the caffeine example, we will want to refer to the means and standard deviations when graphing. Using Excel (or a similar program), follow the same procedure as the prior example, but instead of choosing a Column graph, choose a Line graph.

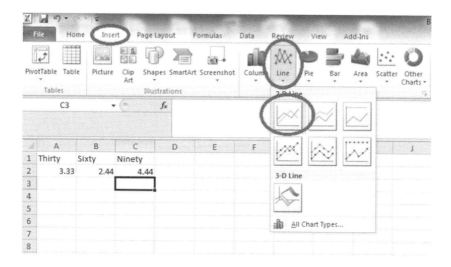

Follow the same procedures as the bar graph (above) until you get to the following semi-formatted graph.

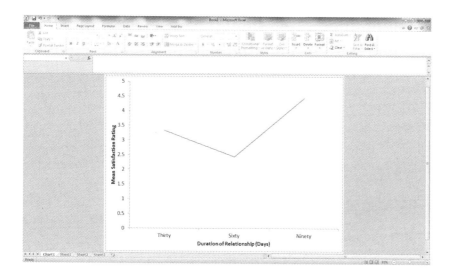

You can see that we need to add error bars and change the line to black. Use the procedure you already know to add error bars. With three conditions in this example, be sure to put the SD values in the top box as well as the bottom box, with each value separated by a comma: 1.00, 0.88, 0.53.

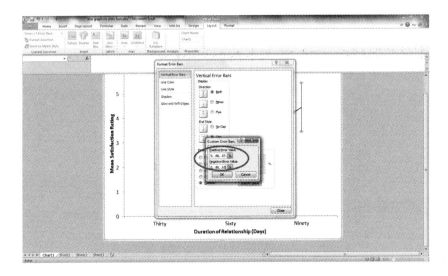

We can also change the width of the data line, if we want to. Finally, we could change the style of the dots above each condition; right now we only see the line connecting three points, but we could make those points into various shapes. Go ahead and use what you already know to change the line to black and add error bars.

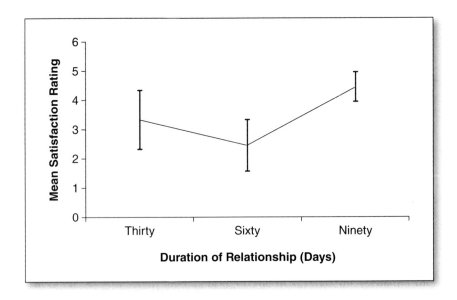

Scatterplots

Line or bar graphs are used when you have clearly separate groups to label the X-axis. The variable might be nominal, ordinal, interval, or ratio data, but you have a few groups of interest that you studied. However, sometimes you will have two interval or ratio variables of interest that are not separated into a few groups, often data you collected in a correlational study. For example, suppose you collected data on length of vacation and enjoyment of the vacation. For the sake of this example, we will just imagine that everyone took a vacation at the same place. If we operationalized length of vacation by days and enjoyment as a rating scale from 1 (terrible) to 6 (wonderful), we can look at some fictional data.

Duration	Enjoyment
4	5
1	3
3	6
2	4
2	3
3	3
4	5
3	5
1	2
4	6
1	2

To create a scatterplot in Excel, simply enter the data as seen above into the Data view. Do not enter the column labels, just the numbers. Or if you want to label the columns to remind you what the columns represent, do not highlight the words; highlight only the numbers.

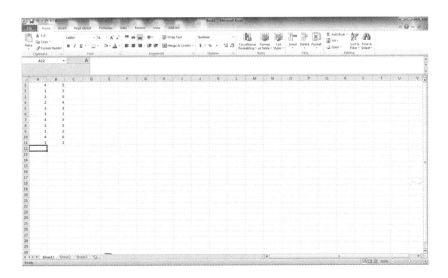

Next click Insert and Scatter, then click on the first scatterplot picture in the upper left corner.

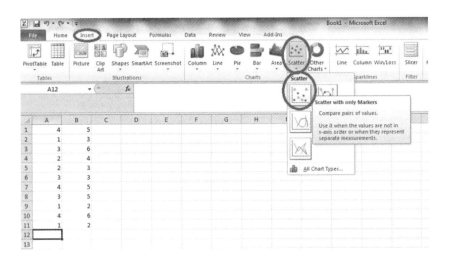

Remember to move the chart to a separate sheet (see instructions earlier in this chapter).

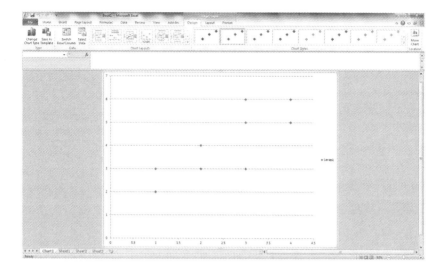

Now we can format the graph using most of the instructions you already know. Right click on one of the many horizontal bars and click Delete. Right click on Series1 and Delete. Change the font sizes of numbers on the X and Y axes, and label the axes. The X-axis is labeled with Duration (we generally use the first column for the X-axis); label the Y-axis with Enjoyment. Notice that we no longer say Mean as part of the Y-axis because a scatterplot is not graphing group means.

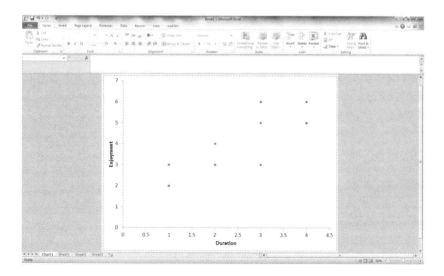

Right click on one of the data points (dots). In the top box that opens, change the dot color to black.

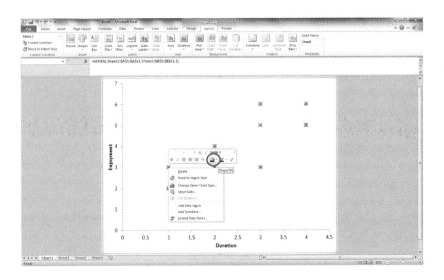

With dots still highlighted, you can change the size and other qualities, if you would like. For a change in size, look at the bottom box (see above) and click Format Data Series. Click Marker Options on the left, then click the circle next to Built-in. Finally, change the marker size to whatever you want. We have chosen to leave them at 7.

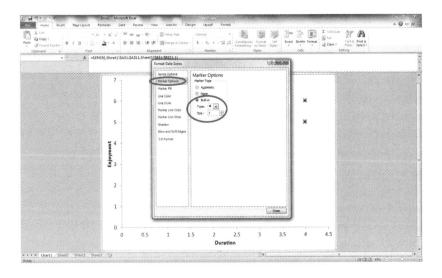

Your graph should look like the scatterplot on the next page.

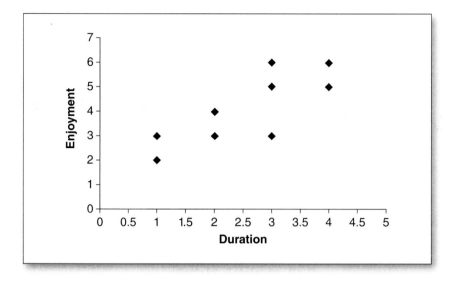

Scatterplotting Regression

If you are predicting the *Y*-axis variable from the *X*-axis variable, or if you simply want to put a line on the graph to show your reader the general trend of the dots, you can click a few more buttons in Excel.

Go to Chart Tools, Layout, Trendline, then click Linear Trendline to show the overall trend of the dot pattern. (Most research relies on linear relationships between variables.)

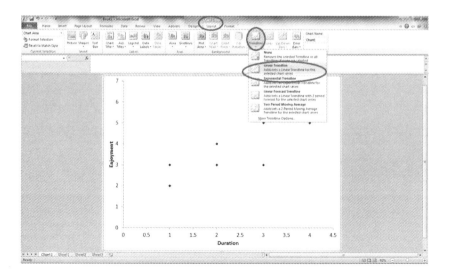

Your new graph should look like the one below. Keep in mind that you can always right click on the line to change the way it looks (e.g., make it thicker).

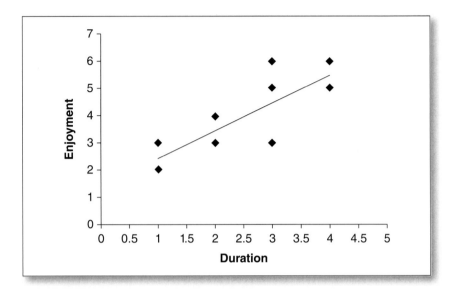

Although we covered graphing in Excel, you should be able to adjust directions for similar software packages. You can also learn more about graphing through coursework such as statistics and research methods as well as in *An EasyGuide to Research Design & SPSS* (Schwartz, B. M., Wilson, J. H., & Goff, D. M., 2015. Thousand Oaks, CA: Sage). No matter how you learn it, learn it! A picture of your data communicates effectively and efficiently, and a poster just looks livelier with a graph.

SECTION III

Oral Presentations

Oral Presentations With PowerPoint 6

As you may have noticed in earlier chapters, an oral presentation is often called a *talk*. We realize this term is simplistic and usually serves as a verb, but people often ask you if you are giving a talk. They are asking if you are speaking in front of a group about your work.

If you have chosen to give a talk, you will need to prepare a formal presentation that includes a visual component, and you will use some type of software. Before we begin, we will admit that several books and websites offer useful information on how to create a presentation; however, one of the main goals of this book is to put everything you need in one place. We generally use PowerPoint, so we focus on that software first, but you can follow the same rules we offer here and use alternative presentation formats. After we cover PowerPoint presentations, we will offer step-by-step instructions on using a free program called Prezi as well as Keynote for Mac users.

Oral-Presentation Format

Getting your thoughts onto presentation software can happen in several ways. For example, you can

- read through your paper and highlight (or bold or underline) key points,
- summarize the main points of each paper section (e.g., introduction, method),

- type your thoughts directly onto the slides, knowing you will fine-tune them after you have a first draft, or
- use some combination of the above or another way we have not considered.

The message here is to get your work from paper format to presentation format. It is always easier to edit a presentation than to stare at a blank page, so get a first draft done as quickly as possible. The background should be white, the fonts should be left at the default setting, and no pictures should be in your presentation. Stylish perks are great, but if you play with those before you have a first draft, you might end up wasting a lot of time to avoid writing the substance of the presentation.

In general, we suggest the following percentage of space spent on each section of your talk.

Title slide/orientation	2%
Introduction	20%
Method	25%
Results	30%
Discussion	20%
Wrap-up slides	3%

Of course the percentages offered above are merely suggestions. If you have never given a talk before, sometimes it helps to have concrete advice. An alternative to this layout is to combine your results and discussion sections. You might present a result or group of results that make sense together, then you can go ahead and speculate why you might have found the outcome(s).

Another deviation from the table above is spending more time on the introduction section. For example, you might be conducting research in a specialized area that requires more explanation in the introduction. Or your talk might summarize a literature review rather than an empirical study. Without a method or results section, you would instead describe your topic and literature review in detail.

Creating a PowerPoint Presentation: Step-by-Step Instructions

Presentation software offers you slides to project onto a white screen or blank wall. You write words on the slides or use other items of visual interest. Of course, if you have adequate computer speakers at a conference, you can even use sound, but audio is not always reliable.

Adding Text

When you open PowerPoint, the software offers you a Title Slide. Put your title, name, affiliation (school), and perhaps the date as well as the name of the conference. We provide examples based on one of our presentations.

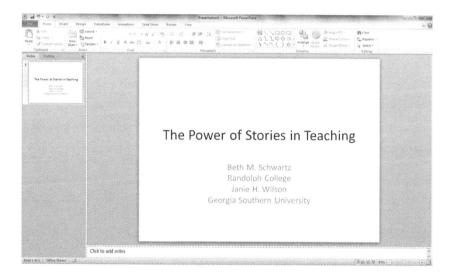

Next, click New Slide at the top of your screen. The program will give you standard slide options, and you can do most things with the Title and Content slide. However, feel free to use other slide formats as needed.

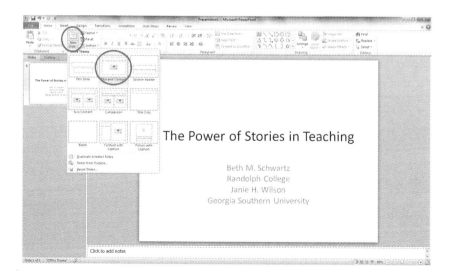

After your Title Slide, the remaining slides are usually Title and Content slides as circled in the previous screenshot.

Refer to the table at the beginning of this chapter for approximate space percentages for each part of your talk. If you are presenting a literature review, divide the talk into meaningful sections based on your paper headings. At this stage in your career, you should type words onto the slides. We know that sounds obvious, but let us explain.

Presentation software was originally designed for a business setting and allowed people to present their work to large audiences. For example, an advertising company might display market research and ad ideas to a group of people to persuade them. In a business setting, it makes sense to offer a lot of information during a presentation. Teachers quickly realized the power of addressing large audiences with technology was far advanced beyond transparencies and overhead projectors. Presentation software is sleek, modern, and allows constant and convenient changes that transparent sheets of paper on an overhead projector do not.

People thought presentation software and the digital age would revolutionize teaching. In some ways it has. But teachers have learned a great deal about tweaking technology to fit the needs of their unique audiences. We now know that busy slides are difficult for students to process, especially since students often take notes during class, dividing their attention between word-laden slides and their own notebooks. To add more chaos to the mix, students have to listen to an instructor lecture, too! Teachers learned a few truths about projection software: (1) Slides should not be too busy, and (2) no one multitasks well.

The revelation that projection software must be used differently in teaching versus business started a wave of changes in the classroom that are still happening today. Based on a lot of excellent research on teaching and learning, we know a good bit about what to do and what not to do as people who want to give away information. You will benefit from that knowledge.

We start with amount of content. Perhaps you have seen presentations that included slides packed with many words. You probably felt overwhelmed by the amount of content as soon as the slide appeared. So here is our first piece of advice: Do not overcrowd a slide with words. Use just enough words to remind you of what to say. The better you get at presentations, the fewer words you will need on the slide. And remember, you are not allowed to read anyway, so why bother projecting entire paragraphs? Let us examine what you should type. The top of the slide has room for a subheading. You already have your title slide, so now maybe you want to use a heading such as Introduction. Then add brief bullet points under the main slide heading.

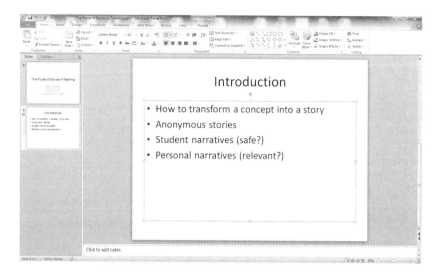

If you want to add a subpoint under a bullet, click Enter and Tab to further indent. If you later decide you did not want to indent, go to the top of the screen and click the button identified below.

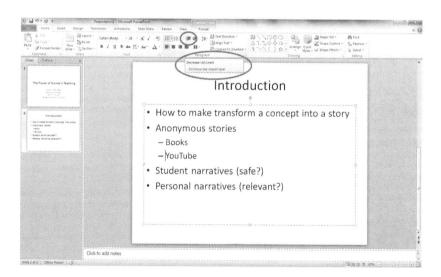

Students usually ask how many slides they should have. That is a tough question to answer because it depends on speed of talking and other aspects of your presentation style. We tend to speak quickly, so we use more slides than most people, with about 15 to 20 slides for a 12 to 13 minute talk. We can get through that many slides in the time allotted. But if you are a slow talker, you are likely to get through fewer slides in the same amount of time. As you practice your presentation, you can get a feel for how many slides you need to stay within the allotted time but not finish too early.

Formatting Your Presentation

When all of your slides have information on them, you can begin to format the slides. It is time for the fun part. You get to play with colors, styles, fonts, and other visual-interest options. Notice that we say visual and not audio. When teachers first started using presentation software, they heavily used the stock sounds that come with PowerPoint. During lecture, students heard squealing brakes, honking horns, applause, and sometimes even breaking glass throughout presentations. Oh, it was terrible! You can only imagine how distracting that was. Every time a new slide was presented, a sound played. Even with all of our knowledge of PowerPoint in teaching, we still hear awful sound effects at conferences and cringe. Our advice? Save the audio for something important, like showing a video clip that clearly demonstrates a tough concept.

Let us begin formatting with decisions about how your slides will change from one to the next. Yes, you get to use some cool transitions, if you would like. But be careful here too; do not set new slides to come in by spinning or zooming. We have heard audience members complain of nausea at the sight of twirling slides. Either set no transitions at all, or set a simple and quick transition such as Cut. If you choose a transition for a slide, you must highlight the slide first. If you want all slides to transition in the same way, left click on the first slide, then Shift + left click on the last slide. Remember to stick with a simple transition. More exciting slide changes are annoying and disorienting. And even a brief lag time when waiting for a slide to change becomes painful after a few slides. Below we have clicked Transitions, then Cut.

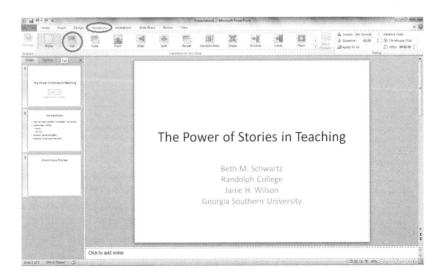

If you do choose a transition, notice the little star that appears on the left side of each slide in the left bar.

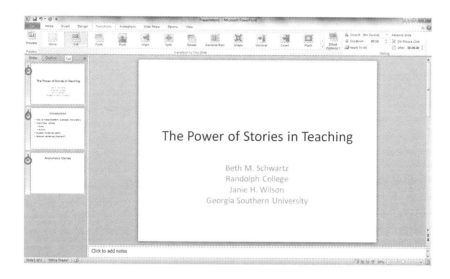

Just as you do not want to distract, bore, or heaven forbid, annoy your viewers with odd slide transitions, you do not want your individual bullet points to flip around as they come on the screen or crawl onto the screen like slugs. If you feel the need to choose a simple way for bullets to enter the screen, click the Animation tab at the top of the screen. In our example, we might highlight the second slide and choose which bullets we want to appear separately by choosing Appear. Highlight words in the bullets to appear individually, usually when you click the mouse during your presentation.

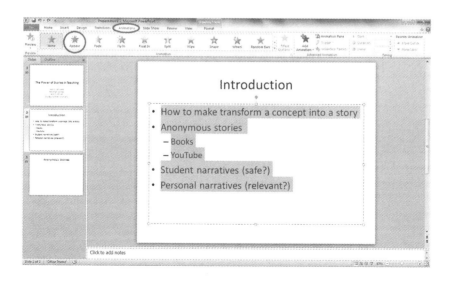

If you click Appear as your option (which is a good choice), you will notice a small number 1 shows up on the left side of each chosen bullet point, as you see in the slide below.

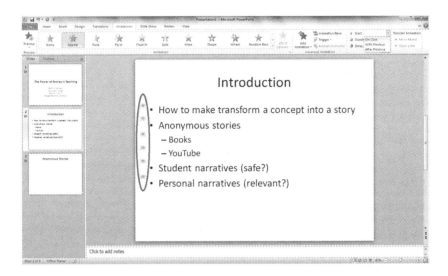

Unfortunately, if you do nothing else, the bullets will all appear on your screen at the same time, so there would be really no point to setting a transition. Speakers usually want to have bullets appear one at a time so they control the pacing of points to be made and focus the audience on one point at a time. With all the information up on the slide, some audience members read ahead and, frankly, do not pay attention to what you are saying. On the top right side of the screen, beside Start, click the down arrow and choose On Click. This option will bring the bullet points in one at a time as you click the mouse during your talk.

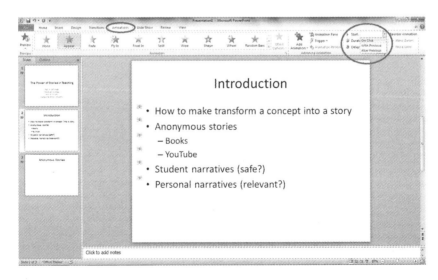

Now you have the content, the transition from one slide to the next, and the bullets within each slide all set for your presentation. As you now sit back and look at your presentation, notice the boring white background. Black words on a white background certainly focus the reader's attention on your message, and the contrast is high, making the presentation highly readable. But wow, that style is no style at all. We suggest at least using one of the simpler styles and adding some color. Click the Design tab at the top of your screen to see options. The example below is Concourse.

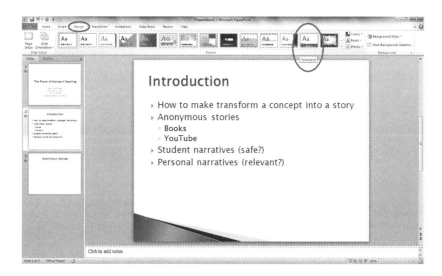

Clicking Concourse (in this example) applies the design to all slides in your presentation; no need to highlight all of the slides in the left bar.

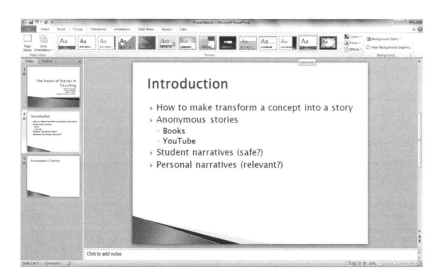

As you gain experience with presentation software and public speaking, you will learn subtleties such as building slides by repeating them and highlighting different parts to focus your audience. In the example below, we repeated slide 2, changed bullets to grey other than the one part we want people to focus on, which we bolded. To create the slideshow view below, we clicked on the icon at the bottom, right of the screen (circled below). Finally, we enlarged the slides by moving the size option to the right (also circled on the bottom right side of the screen).

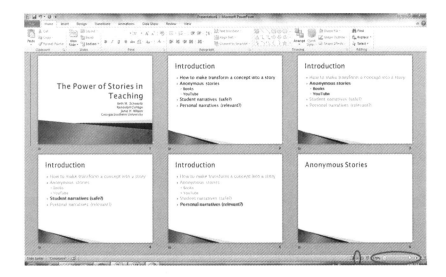

Adding Nontext Materials

Now let us get really crazy and suggest inserting a figure or two (or more) into your presentation. If you have a results section, you should insert a graph, if relevant (see Chapter 5). Or you might choose to insert a picture. An example would be showing a piece of equipment from the lab or a stimulus that you used in your study. We will use a random .jpg file from our collection (see next page).

To insert this picture, we will continue with the same slideshow we were creating. Insert a New Slide. PowerPoint will give you another slide with the same layout you have been using, and this layout is fine. In fact, most of the layouts have the same six icons (see the center of the next screen) that allow you to insert pictures, charts, and so on. In this case, we click on the picture icon as seen below.

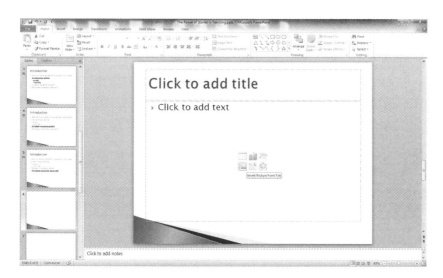

Insert the picture from the correct location when your computer directory opens. When the picture appears on your slide, resize it by clicking and pulling the borders with your mouse.

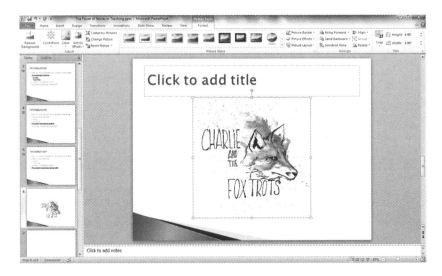

You also can move the entire picture around on the side and play with formatting options at the top of your computer screen. Finally, add a title at the top of the slide if you want a title, and insert text boxes (see Chapter 4 for how to insert text boxes) on the slide as needed.

We admit that an easier way to insert images is to copy the image from its original location, right click somewhere on your PowerPoint slide, and click Paste when the options box opens. Done.

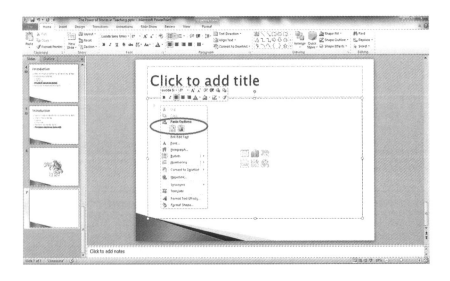

This simpler approach also works well to insert tables and graphs. Yes, icons to insert tables and graphs are located on the slide, but we merely copy a graph we want to use and paste it on the slide. For an example using one of the graphs from Chapter 5, see below.

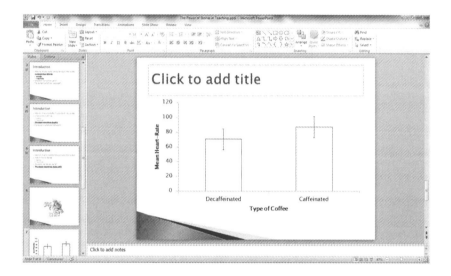

Figures make your presentation more interesting, but they must be relevant. Pictures of you and your friends on spring break are not likely to be relevant. If they are, by all means use them! Just be sure the figures tie to your talk. Do not be concerned that the pictures are necessary to understand your presentation; they might just provide visual interest. As long as the visual interest does not cause people to mentally wander from your talk, use the image. A final caution: Do not overdo it with too many figures. You still should follow the rule of keeping the presentation simple and clear. Also remember you have to discuss the figure, which carries a time cost. Because the figure and graph we added above have nothing to do with the presentation, we will delete them now by right clicking on each slide and choosing Cut on the menu that opens.

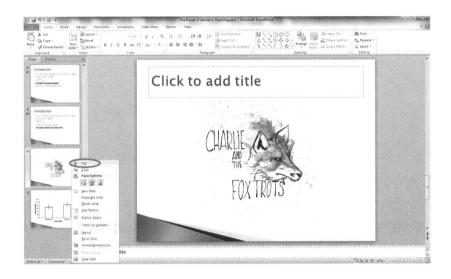

Another fun option we use when teaching classes is to add links, such as a web address for a YouTube video. Inserting internet links is easy. Type or copy a link into a slide, and test it out by beginning the slideshow on that slide. Click the link. If you have a reliable internet connection, the link works automatically. As informative as these links can be for a presentation, we do not suggest using this feature at a conference where connection may be unavailable, lost in the middle of a presentation, or just slow. For an in-class presentation or where you know you have a reliable internet connection, using links is not a problem. At a conference, you could consider placing the video clip on your computer and bringing your computer to use for your presentation. Bring cords and connectors too!

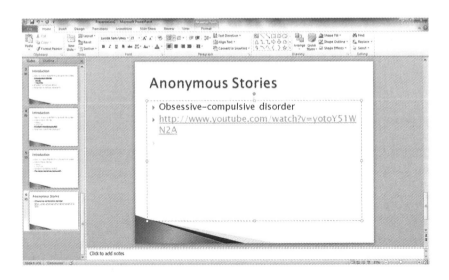

Get Ready, Set, Start the Show

When you are ready to start the slideshow, click on the first slide, then click the icon on the bottom right of the screen that looks like a pull-down projection screen (circled below).

Recall that earlier we said teachers have learned to adjust presentation software to meet the needs of their audiences. But we address more than one type of audience. Teachers work with students, and the goal is to teach new information to be tested later. A second type of audience is found at conferences. When we offer a presentation, we focus on the audience, which requires us to adjust our presentation and our style. When the audience is our students, we prepare PowerPoint slides with a lot of visual interest, links to YouTube, and very few words. In fact, we often try to use no words at all. Relevant pictures can replace words, and pictures remind the presenter what needs to be covered. Students are not left floundering as they try to listen to the instructor, read slides, and take notes from the slides. After all, multitasking is a myth. All we can really do is serial tasking, and the best we can hope for is quickly changing from one task to another. Constantly changing our cognitive focus impairs learning. So as teachers, we stick with visual interest and engaging students' attention.

However, when we present at a conference, we know our audience is different. We know these are our peers, and they have a foundation of knowledge similar to our own. We also know audience members will not be tested later. They do not need to feverishly take notes to prepare for an assessment. They want to sit back and learn about something new or think about an old idea in a new way. And because audience members are already motivated to listen and watch, we do not spend as much effort to engage them as we would with students who perhaps are taking the course because it is a requirement. At conferences, PowerPoint slides have more words, fewer pictures, and almost no audio (unless the audio is crucial to the topic). We rarely rely on an internet connection, and given the time constraints, we usually cannot include demonstrations or activities to maintain audience interest.

As you can see, different audiences call for different approaches. And both of these teaching approaches are a bit different from the business approaches that started this revolution. But where does that leave you? You fall in the middle. You are presenting in class or to a conference audience, so you can assume some basic knowledge of your topic. Use words, but remember that words might become a burden if your goal later is to *teach* the material to people who have little or no background. And recognize that visual interest on your PowerPoint slides might make the presentation more interesting to *you*.

Prezi Presentations 7

An Alternative to PowerPoint

M ost people currently use PowerPoint slides for oral presentations. However, a second popular option is Prezi.com. This site is free and offers a different approach to presentations. A *Prezi* allows more creative control, relying on a one-page workspace to design elements of your presentation. When preparing for your talk, you will need to decide which part of the workspace to zoom in on first, second, and so on. The path (order) of what Prezi zooms in on is the order of your presentation. PowerPoint offers a sequence of slides, with one slide presented after another; Prezi offers one big picture, and you decide the order in which the program zooms in on different parts of the picture. In addition to more creative control, a Prezi constantly reminds the viewer of the big picture by moving across the entire workspace as it zooms from one component to another. We can use eating a meal as an analogy. PowerPoint is like a meal brought out to you in separate courses, one after the other. Prezi is like a buffet, placing all courses in front of you at once. For either type of meal, you still focus on one bite at a time.

Creating a Prezi: Step-by-Step Instructions

Let us show you how to create a simple Prezi. First, you will need to create an account. Go to the Prezi.com website. There you will see the following screen. Click "Sign up now" on the bottom of the screen.

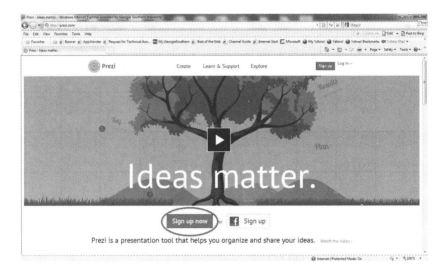

Next click the Public option on the left. It is free!

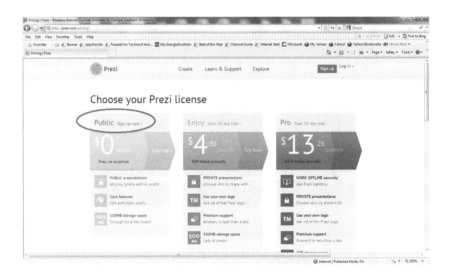

Create an account by completing your information on the form, then click Sign up.

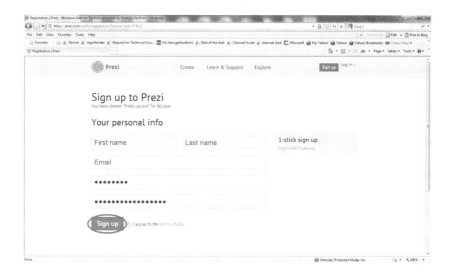

After you have an account, you will Log in by clicking the upper right button on the screen (see the sample screen below). A box will show you where to type your e-mail. Your password goes in the box below the e-mail, but the box will appear to already have your password in it as indicated by dots. Click into that space to remove the dots and type your actual password. Choose Log in near the bottom of the screen.

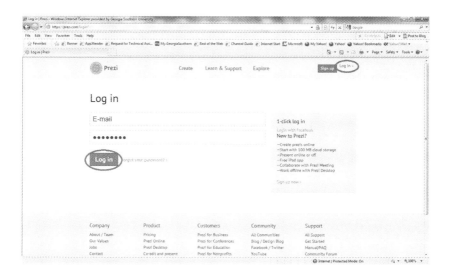

After you enter your information and choose Log in, click on New Prezi on the left side of the page.

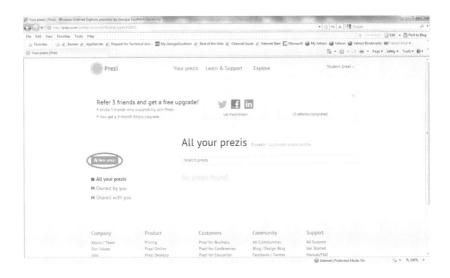

Adding Text

Several options will be available to you. These slide designs are similar to designs found in PowerPoint, but Prezi designs are a bit more playful (see below).

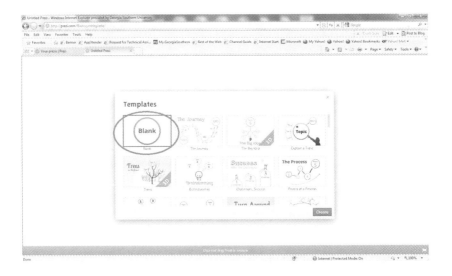

The creative themes offered by Prezi are fun, but we will focus our discussion on the plain, ordinary blank presentation. As indicated above, click the upper left presentation with the circle on it (Blank). The following screen will appear.

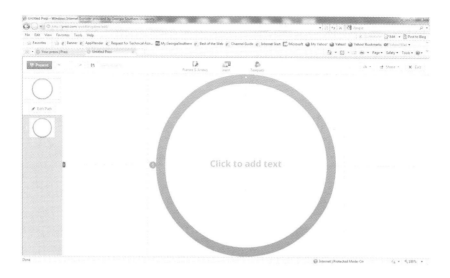

We will not work with this circle yet. Instead, we will begin to build a presentation by clicking Frames and Arrows near the top center of the screen. This icon opens a box with several options.

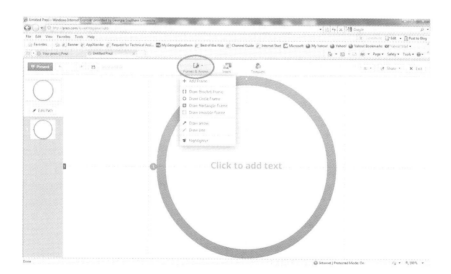

To keep our approach simple, you can click the + button that says Add Frame at the top of the menu. We can always change the format of the added frame later. Notice below that a Bracket Frame appears to the right of the circle frame already on the screen.

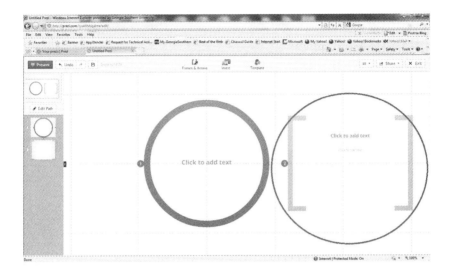

Formatting Your Presentation

Click anywhere on the grey bracket to see a few options appear. These options will allow you to zoom in, change the format of the bracket (such as to a rectangle), or change the size of the frame.

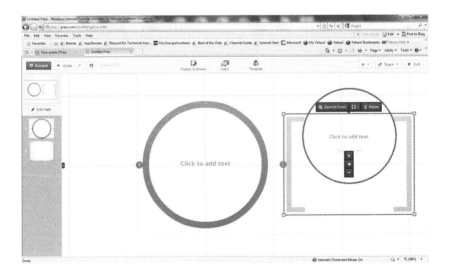

We will use a rectangle on this presentation, so click beside the bracket picture above the frame and choose Rectangle.

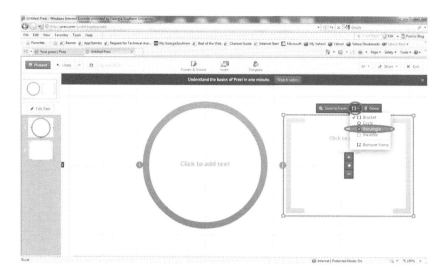

The background of the rectangle turned blue, but we would rather have grey. Right click on the rectangle icon above your frame and choose Change background to play with colors. Please note that this option will only show up if you right click on the [ ] icon above the slide.

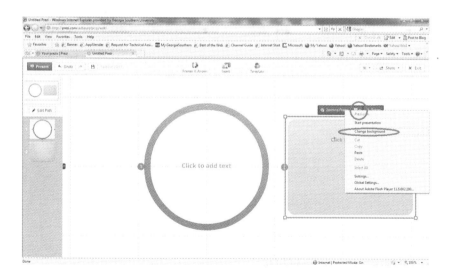

The color of the overall workspace is white, and that seems fine, so choose Next at the bottom of the screen in the middle.

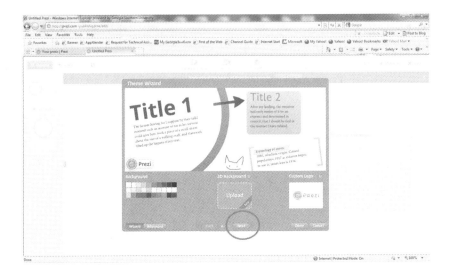

The second screen (see below) allows you to adjust various fonts. You might want to play with these options later, but for now we are still looking for the box or slide background color. Click Next again.

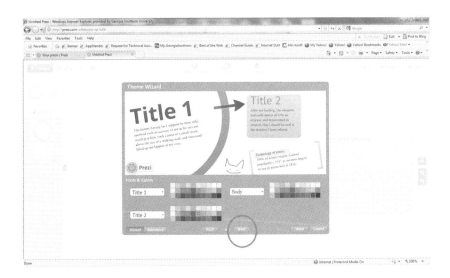

Finally, we can see an option for Bracket Frame and Rectangle on the bottom left side. Click grey and Done on a screen that looks like the one on the next page.

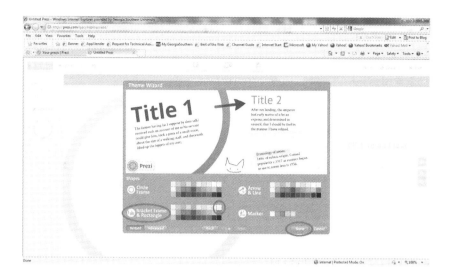

On the next screenshot, we show you how to start typing in the box. Adding text is easy because the box already has spaces set up for you to type. If you do not like the size or location of text boxes, you can change it later. Click into one of the boxes and start typing. The larger box at the top defaults to a title size; the one below it defaults to a subtitle size. You can click for a different size, font, and color as needed.

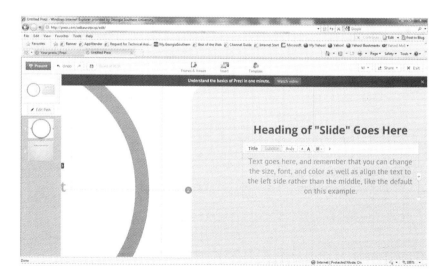

Click anywhere outside of the slide box (rectangle) to get an idea of how the slide looks.

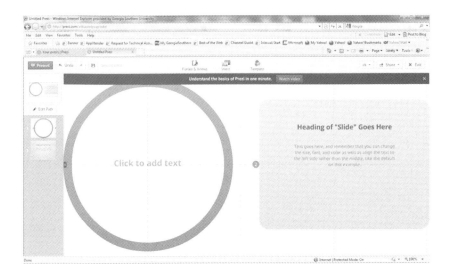

Even better, zoom out to see how the entire presentation (or Prezi board) looks. Move your cursor to the right edge of the screen. Click the home icon with the house on it. Prezi will zoom out and show you the entire workspace. Notice the two other icons on the right that help you zoom in or out. Rolling the scroll button on your mouse will also zoom.

We can go ahead and add more Frame Brackets, and for the sake of this beginning tutorial, we will continue to click the + icon offered by Frames and Arrows. Prezi puts the new brackets in reasonable locations, but of course you can always move them around later. (We will leave our sample slide where it was, but you would move it to a relevant location in a real presentation.)

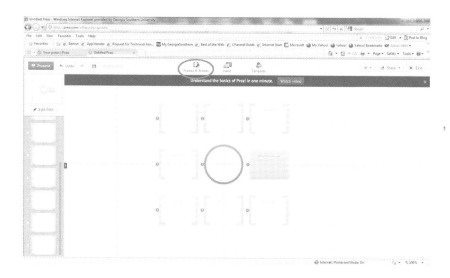

We might want to start adding details in the upper left corner. Perhaps we would put the abstract there. We will change the bracket to a rectangle and make it grey.

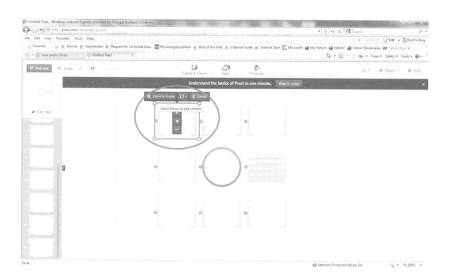

Then we would type a Title and Subtitle. If you ever want to add another text box on the workspace, simply double click, and the program will provide one.

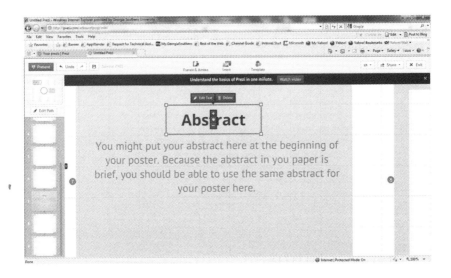

So far, below is what our entire workspace looks like if we click the Home icon on the right (after moving the cursor to that side of the screen).

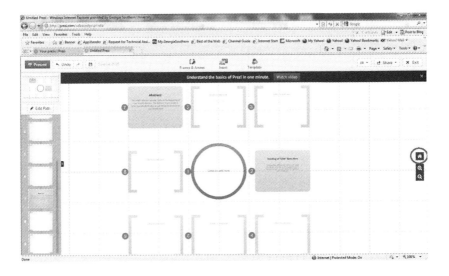

Maybe your next step would be to summarize the introduction from your paper. If you need a larger rectangle, click on it and pull the corner to resize.

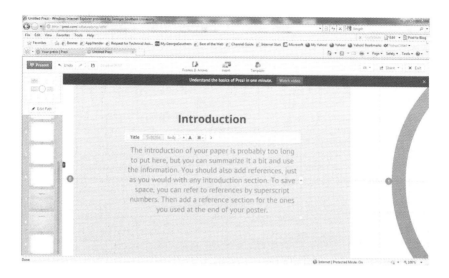

Adjust your view as needed to get a better look at the slide.

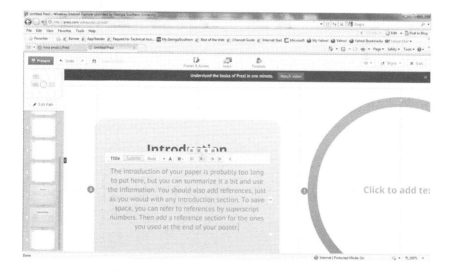

Follow the same procedure for the method section.

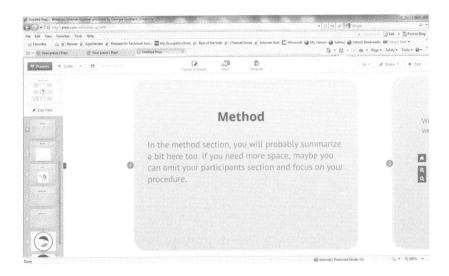

We will skip the results section for right now and come back to it in a bit, but we can go ahead and add a discussion slide.

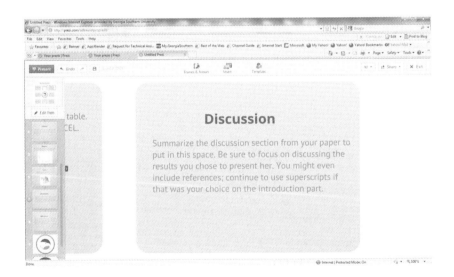

And you should include a slide for key references used in your presentation.

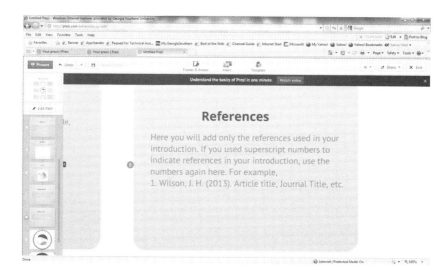

We saved results for last because you might want to add more than text. First, type in a results title, adding text as needed and then clicking the box and dragging it to a good location on the slide. Remember that you can also resize with the plus or minus buttons or simply drag the corner of the text box.

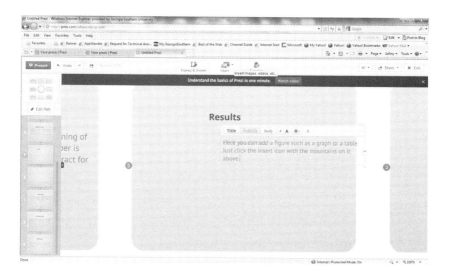

Adding Nontext Materials

A good way to display results is using a graph or table. To insert a graph, for example, we find it easiest to copy the graph (such as from Excel) and paste it here. We have chosen a random graph to insert for the sake of example. Prezi will show you that it is working on pasting the graph, and this process might take a bit of time.

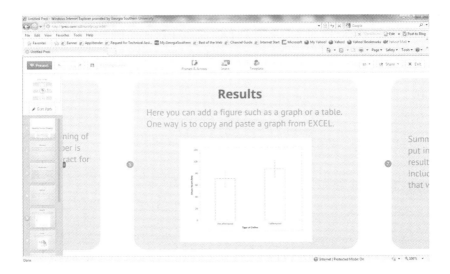

You might also want to insert an image by clicking the Insert button and choosing Image.

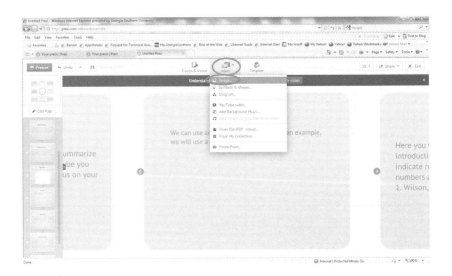

The following box will open, allowing you to select files by clicking that button. You have the option of searching for public images, but we generally rely on our own pictures.

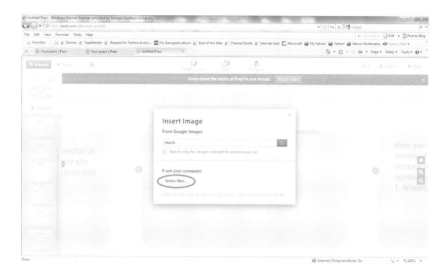

From your computer files, choose the file you want to insert. Although Prezi might take a bit of time to insert the picture, the program will tell you it is working on it. When it appears, resize and move the image as needed.

For fun, let us return to the center of the workspace again. We chose to leave the center slide in that space and as a circle because we have a lovely circular logo to insert. Now we zoom to that center slide, click Insert and Image, and insert the logo. We wait briefly while Prezi works.

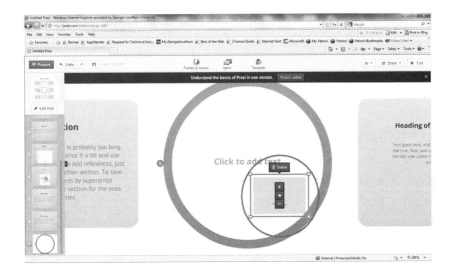

The logo is inserted in that same location.

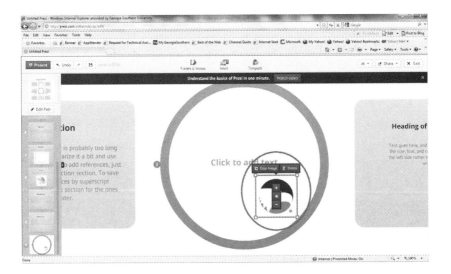

We enlarge the image and move it to the center.

Now we click the Home icon on the right of the screen again to see what our workspace looks like.

It looks good! Of course we need a title, and we can add one by double clicking in any part of the workspace we want to use. If you have trouble moving around in the screen (maybe you need more space above the rectangles), right click onto a blank area of the workspace, do not release the click, and move the entire workspace around. Notice that we have added three text boxes at the top of the work area and then adjusted size and location for our title, names, and affiliation.

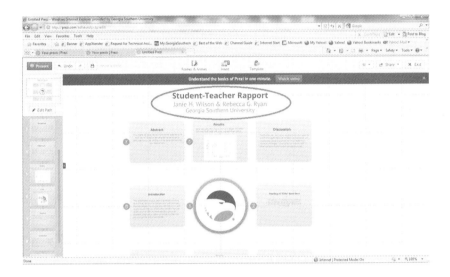

Get Ready, Set, Start the Show

So far we have modeled our presentation based on the major sections of an empirical study, but this approach was just to give us a starting place. If you decide to create something more visually interesting, all you need to do is let Prezi know which slides to zoom in on, and in what order. Prezi calls this a *path*. Click Edit Path on the left of the screen. Numbers in circles will appear beside slides in the workspace. Click and drag the numbers around so you can choose the order of slide presentation. Or look on the left side of the screen; simply click and drag the slides to place them in whatever order you like. If a slide on your workspace is not seen on the left or has no number beside it on the workspace, click the slide in the workspace once to copy it to the left bar. In the end, the order of slides in the left sidebar is the path order for your presentation.

Notice the logical path for our following presentation. We start with our title and move from there through the presentation. We did not include our playful sample slide from the very beginning of this chapter because we used it just to introduce Prezi. Of course, if you created a Prezi, you would want to delete irrelevant slides from your workspace.

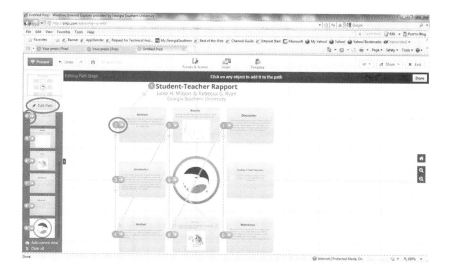

Notice above that the final link in the path is to end on our center slide. For added drama, we can click only on the logo picture file in the center, creating a final link in our pathway. After Prezi moves to the middle slide, the next step will be to zoom in on the eagle logo.

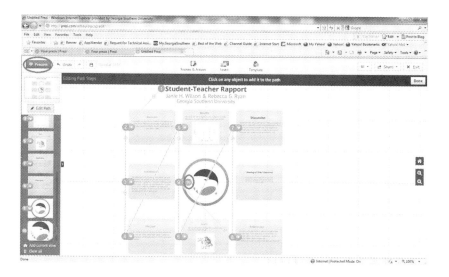

To begin using this Prezi as an oral presentation, click the Present button in the upper left corner when you are ready to begin (see above). As shown on the next page, the first zoom will show the first link in the path.

Student-Teacher Rapport
Janie H. Wilson & Rebecca G. Ryan
Georgia Southern University

As a final caution, whether you are using traditional PowerPoint or the newer option, Prezi, keep it simple. Sure, you will want to include graphs and other figures, and a video can be useful, but do not overwhelm your audience. With PowerPoint, many presenters go way too far with the glitz, adding screeching car tires and slowly crawling text. With Prezi, presenters might be tempted to zoom around the workspace quickly or even add effects that we did not cover here. Members of your audience may get dizzy from too much zooming and spinning. Regardless of the platform you choose, make your presentation interesting but not annoying.

We have presented the basics of Prezi here, and even the basics can be accomplished in more than one way. Play with Prezi to see what you can create. Do not limit yourself to rectangles. Perhaps circles look better, or maybe you will want to remove borders completely. You are not restricted to a linear look when organizing your message. Also think about the pathway between elements. The Prezi is newer and creatively different from PowerPoint, but both are excellent choices for oral presentations.

Keynote Presentations 8

Slides for Mac

In addition to PowerPoint and Prezi, another software package available to create slides for oral presentations is Keynote 2009. Interestingly, this software package was originally developed by Apple in order for Steve Jobs to give flashy presentations at the Macworld Conference and Expo. Of course, he did not want to present his innovative new devices using PowerPoint, a Microsoft product. So obviously, the application (usually referred to as *software*) was developed for Mac. This chapter describes Keynote 2009 for Mac computers. Keynote is part of the iWorks package, which also contains software for other needs such as documents and spreadsheets. For mobile devices, you can purchase a Keynote application available for use on iPhones, iPods, or iPads. The mobile application is a bit different, but knowing Keynote 2009 should allow you to learn how to use the mobile-device application pretty quickly.

This chapter covers the basics, allowing you to get started and even add some eye-catching effects to your presentation. Throughout the chapter, we explain the purpose of many items on the Keynote toolbar, and as always, we provide screenshots to guide you. As is true for any software, there are many options and choices to consider that will make your slides more attractive. Here we stick to the *EasyGuide* philosophy of sticking to the basics. After you become familiar with Keynote, you can consider the additional options available. As with the presentation software discussed in earlier chapters, you need to avoid overdoing it with transitions or animations. You never want these parts of your presentation to distract from the message you are trying to convey to the audience. People should walk away knowing about the content of your talk rather than remember how exciting the slides were that flew across the screen or how distracting the text was that sparkled in your slides.

Creating a Keynote Presentation: Step-by-Step Instructions

To get started with Keynote, you need to choose a theme for your presentation. The Theme Chooser options will first appear when you open the software. Similar to PowerPoint, when you choose a theme it will be used throughout your document. This means that choosing at theme provides a consistent style of text, colors, and text boxes throughout.

The screenshot of the toolbar below shows you which icon to click if you want to return to themes later.

Adding Text

After you choose a theme and double-click on that choice, a title page will open. As you see in the example on the next page, the format of the title page provides a space for your title and your name.

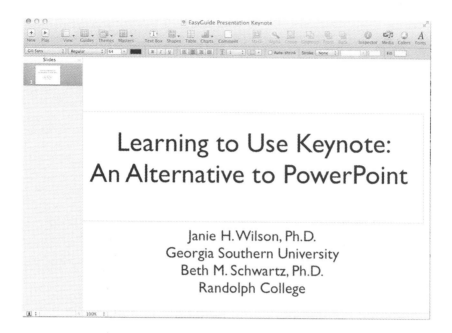

To add new slides, click New at the top left (circled below) on the toolbar.

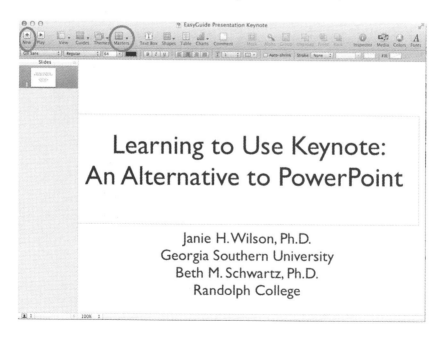

Further, clicking Masters (also circled above) will open a drop-down menu as shown in the next screenshot. Several options allow you to include text, images, a blank slide, and so on. For each new slide, you can decide the format that best meets your needs.

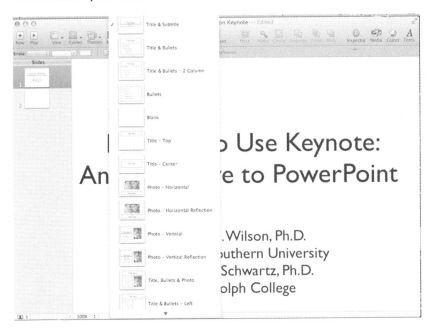

After you have established the look of the slide, use the text placeholder that says "Double-click to edit" to add text as needed.

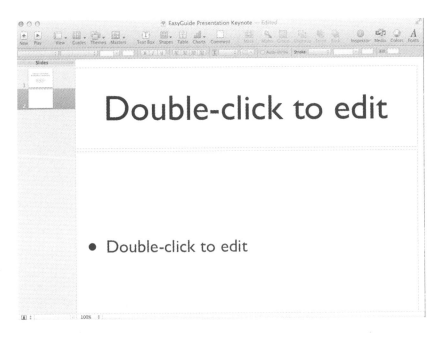

Similar to PowerPoint, many choices are available to format your text. Look beneath the main toolbar for text format options. Notice in the circles below that you can change the type of font, font size, and format of your text. When clicking on each section, all available options will appear in a drop-down menu.

As you build your presentation, you may want to view it in various ways. The View icon (circled below) allows you to choose how you want the screen to appear.

Below are the many choices you have from the View icon. First we examine Navigator view.

In this view, each time you add a new slide, it is added to the slide navigator displayed to the left of the screen (a sidebar). The size of the slides in the slide navigator can be changed using the options at the bottom left of the screen. Click that icon (circled below at the far left), and you can choose between small, medium, and large icons in the navigator. In addition, the slides can be rearranged easily, and the size of the slide view can be altered using the icon circled below marked 100%. Experiment with the different ways to organize slides and decide what works best for your presentation.

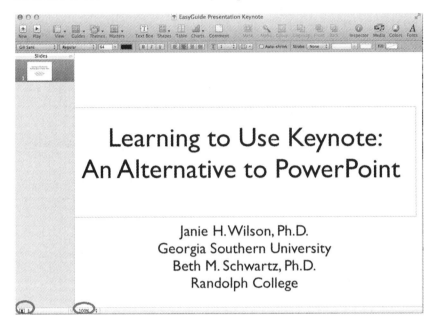

The other option for View is to choose the second option on the menu: Outline.

This option will include bulleted text from your slides instead of a miniversion of your slides in the sidebar.

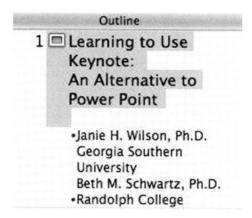

If you would rather see all of your slides where the larger slide usually appears, choose the Light Table option under the View menu.

With this option you can see all of your slides and can perhaps more easily rearrange the order.

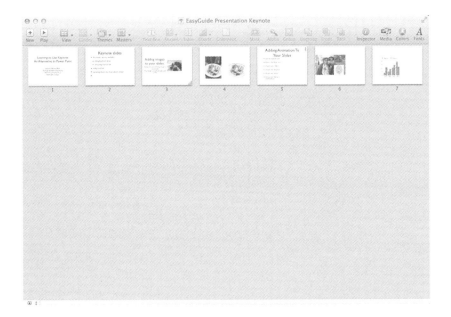

You can also view the slide in full screen by choosing the Slide Only option from the menu.

Now you can view your slides just as they would appear on the screen during your presentation.

We generally prefer the View of Navigator because we can see the larger slide as well as the sequence of all slides on the left (see the next screenshot).

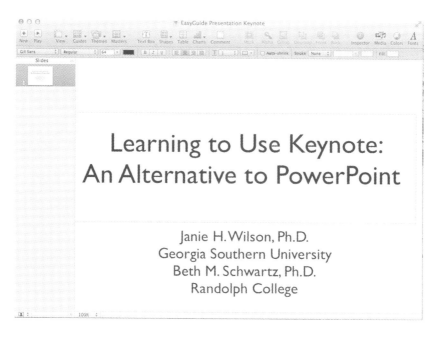

Formatting Your Presentation

After you add all your slides, you can consider an abundance of formatting options of including transitions to new slides. In fact, far too many options are available to cover here. We suggest that you open Keynote and see how to add transition effects such as Shimmer, Doorway, Flip, and Flop. These names probably seem odd, but they will make more sense when you play with Keynote options (see below). A number of transitions offered through Keynote 2009 are not available using PowerPoint or Prezi. For instance, using Magic Move you can include the same picture in two consecutive slides, moving the image from one slide to the next with the appearance of the image moving across the screen. The best way to choose transitions is to open your presentation and pick the one that fits best with your presentation. These options are found when choosing the Inspector icon from the toolbar.

Next click on the second icon that looks like a slide (circled below). You will see the word Slide appear in the box above all the icons. Click Transition to reveal options.

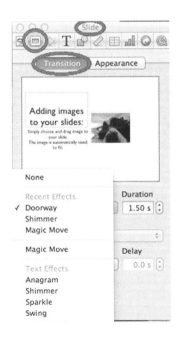

In addition to having slides appear in an interesting (but not overwhelming) way, you might want to include text on your slide one section at a time. This way you can help the audience focus on the point you are making rather than read ahead. To add movement or animation, use the Inspector tool, and choose the diamond-shaped icon as seen below to open the options called Build in Keynote.

The Build option allows you to decide many details about how you animate the text, including the speed of your animation (see Duration below).

Of course Keynote does not restrict you to text. You can add many other components to your slides, and you can animate each one as you choose.

Adding Nontext Materials

If you want to include media such as photos, audio, or movies, use the Media icon.

You will see three options across the top of the window that appears. First, let us talk about adding an image. To add an image, choose the Photos option from the Media window. You can see in the next screen shot that the different photo files on your computer will appear in the window.

To add any of these images, simply click on the image and drag it to the slide. Keynote will automatically size the image and fit it for the format included in the particular slide format you selected. Then you can make changes to the picture itself if you choose to do so.

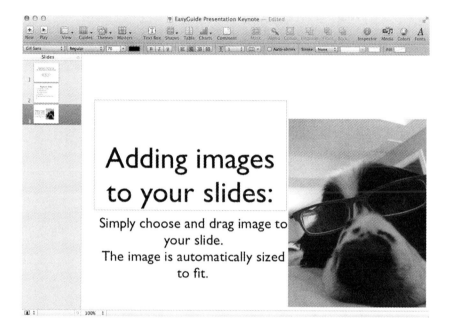

If you like the image, but the background is distracting, change the background using the graphics tool located at the Alpha icon.

After clicking the Alpha icon, place the mouse over the background color you want to remove from the image. Click on the part of the background you want to make transparent and then drag the mouse to remove additional background of the same color. You can do this to all of the different colors in the background to remove everything behind your image. Look at the example on the next page. The Alpha tool was used many times in the image to remove the numerous background colors behind the image.

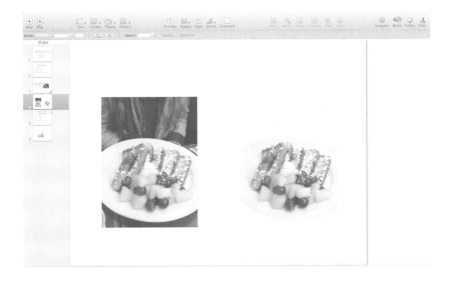

Notice that when working with images, the second format bar across the top of your screen changes from the options we used to format text. Here you can choose, for example, the borders, brightness, and shadows for your image.

It is also easy to crop and resize images for your presentation by using the Mask icon from the toolbar.

First, click on the image and then choose Mask. A box will appear that allows you to crop the image. Then resize the image by using your mouse on the small window that appears below the image and provides a zooming slide bar.

If you want your presentation to be more engaging, you can easily insert audio and video. To add a song or an image, open the media browser in the toolbar (the same one you used to add an image).

You can then choose the Audio option. There you will see audio files to include from sources such as GarageBand or iTunes. Any audio files you have on your computer will appear in the Media window when you choose Audio as illustrated in the next screenshot. (Yes, we know the songs shown below are oldies but goodies.)

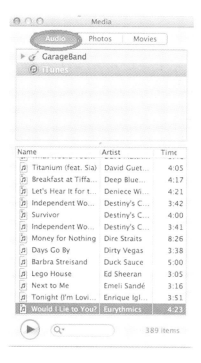

You can click on each file to preview. After you decide which audio to include in your presentation, drag the file to the slide where you want to add the audio. Drag the item by clicking on it with the left side of the mouse and holding the click until you have moved the file. An audio icon will appear on your slide, though it will not be visible when you show your presentation to an audience.

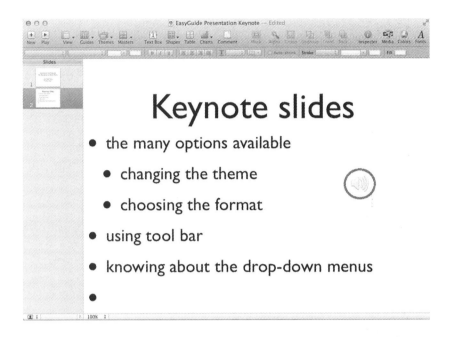

Click on the icon, and choose Inspector from the toolbar. The following window will appear so you can adjust the volume as needed. It is important to note that since the volume for your presentation will be controlled by your computer and by the external audio source, check the volume before your presentation to avoid any embarrassing volume mishaps.

When you get to this slide in your presentation, the audio will automatically begin to play.

We assume that many of you likely use PowerPoint more often than Keynote. Fortunately, Keynote is compatible with PowerPoint, so documents can be imported and exported between each type of software. If you already have a document prepared in PowerPoint, you could save it in iCloud or DropBox, open it in Keynote on your Mac or mobile device, and then show slides by connecting your MacBook or mobile device to an available projector.

Get Ready, Set, Start the Show

If you are presenting your work at a conference, you might end up using someone else's computer, and the computer may be a PC with PowerPoint. Not to worry, you can save your Keynote presentation as a PowerPoint file and bring the compatible file with you. Choose the Export option under File, and then choose PPT.

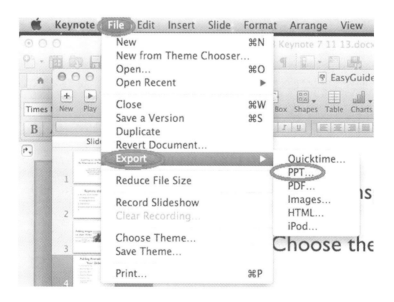

The following window will appear, allowing you to choose the format of the exported file.

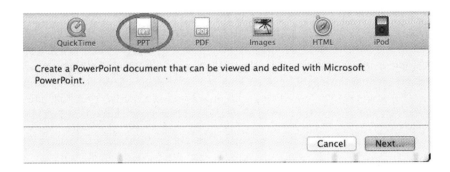

Next you will be asked where you want the exported file to end up. In the screenshot below, we chose to export the file in PowerPoint to the desktop.

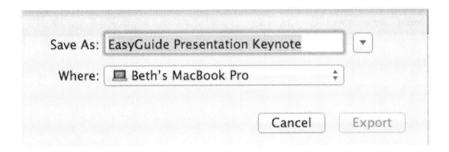

Another option you can choose is the Share option. When you choose Share, you can then choose Send via mail (i.e., e-mail) or the .PPT option.

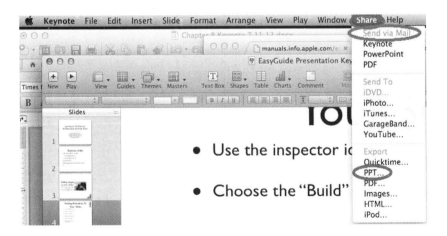

When you choose Send via mail, pick the type of file you want to e-mail (i.e., Keynote, PowerPoint, or PDF). You will be prompted to type in the email address of the receiver. Or you can choose the Export option, also available here, and then choose .PPT. Keep in mind that some of the options you included in your Keynote presentation might not be supported in PowerPoint (e.g., Masking), which means you could lose some of your formatting when you save and send a Keynote file. When you choose the .PPT option to export, a window will appear to let you know what parts of your presentation might be changed.

If instead you created a presentation in PowerPoint and want to open it in Keynote, all you need to do is drag the file to the Keynote icon on your screen or simply open the PowerPoint file in Keynote. When you are ready to show your presentation using Keynote, choose Play.

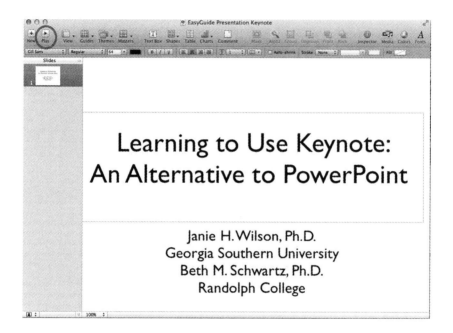

Slides will appear on your computer screen in the same format as the audience sees. However, Keynote offers a useful feature that allows you to see a different layout on your computer screen. Although your audience will see a single slide, Keynote can show you (the presenter) many features, such as the slide, notes, and a timer for your talk. Choose Customize Presenter Display, which is an option available under Play as shown below.

Using this option allows you to create a display for your eyes only. You can also rearrange the display by clicking and dragging each component to a different place on the screen. When you like the arrangement, click Done (circled below).

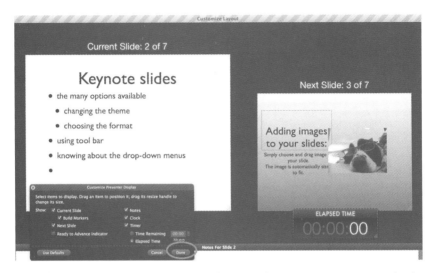

We have zoomed in on the lower left box to show your options more clearly.

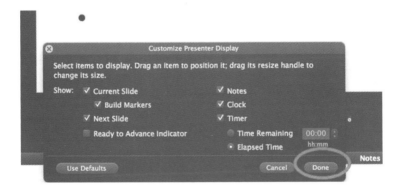

When you click Play, you will see the more detailed screen that you have set up. Remember, your audience will not be able to see what is on your computer screen; only slides will be visible to audience members.

We have presented the basics here, with the *EasyGuide* focused on including essential information to allow you to create a presentation using Keynote 2009. Obviously there is more to learn, and by accessing the over 200 pages in the online Keynote manual, the information is at your fingertips. You might find that Keynote is your favorite presentation software and want to learn all the possible options. And if you are a Mac enthusiast, Keynote is probably the presentation format for you.

Effective Oral Presentations 9

Preparing for Your Performance

In Chapters 6, 7, and 8, you learned how to write a presentation using software for that purpose. In this chapter, we assume you have written a good presentation, which of course is the first step toward preparing for your talk. Now that you have a top-notch presentation, we will cover the need to change it! How will you know that your presentation still needs work? Read on.

Practice

You already know that we want you to practice. Practice does not really make perfect, but it makes a task much, much better, and as we mentioned in Chapter 3, you will be much less anxious if you feel more prepared. Sometimes students believe they perform better under pressure and choose not to practice their talks after writing them. And we have seen the results of such a belief. Ouch. Now we insist that our students practice in spite of how convinced they might be that their presentation will suffer. Even those of us who have given numerous talks still practice over and over again. This time should be set aside not only to practice the talk itself but also to figure out the questions you are likely to be asked and how you will respond to those questions.

When you practice, be sure to practice the entire talk. Often, students practice the first part of the talk many times but neglect to practice the whole talk. Or students avoid sections they are not comfortable presenting. It is easy to avoid what we are least confident about in our talk; fear decreases when we turn away from discomfort. Conquer your fear, and practice difficult sections. Overpractice them. As a result, you will not get tripped up during your talk, sputtering nonsense while anxiety grows.

Practicing comes in several forms:

- Read over the slides on your computer, thinking about what you might want to say when each slide is projected.
- Say out loud what you are thinking while still relaxing in front of your computer.
- Project your slides on a wall, and discuss your slides aloud to yourself.
- Add a friend as your audience during the mock presentation.
- Ask your instructor to serve as your audience.
- Do the entire presentation for people who know something about your topic, such as your class.

Notice that for most of the practice options above, we recommend that you actually speak the talk out loud. Why? We have had the experience of students who give a talk that goes over the time limit, and then they explain afterward that they had practiced and timed it often. The problem was the practice was in their head and not out loud. Speaking a talk takes significantly more time than going over the talk in your head. The simple act of moving your mouth and making the sounds is time consuming. Hence, you need to practice giving your talk by speaking it to either no one or to someone who will provide honest feedback. That type of practice can help ensure that your talk will be the appropriate length. Although it might go without saying, be sure to get feedback from others early in the process when you still can make changes and improve the presentation. We urge you, in particular, to get early feedback from your instructor. Few teaching experiences are more frustrating than offering expert and well-meaning advice to a student who asks for it—and then does not incorporate the feedback! Make time to adjust your talk after you get instructor suggestions.

Often, research includes a team working together to complete the project. Therefore, you might be in a situation in which you conducted research with others. This collaboration means the presentation will be divided among the two or sometimes three of you on the research team. Our word of advice with multiple presenters is to divide the talk equally among the presenters, but be sure to transition at an appropriate place in your talk even if it means that one presenter talks for a bit longer than others. You will not be surprised that the best place for transitioning from one presenter to the next is when you are finished discussing your hypotheses and are about to start presenting your method. Or perhaps the timing works best to transition after the method and before results. Again, transitions will depend on the content of your talk. Just keep in mind that you want to transition only once between copresenters; do not attempt to trade off slides. It is distracting and time consuming to have people come back and forth to the podium throughout the talk. Present your portion and then step aside for the next presenter. All of this must be practiced to make sure the talk and transitions will run smoothly.

Make Notes for Yourself

Whether you are practicing for an individual presentation or a group talk, practice in most or all the ways we suggested earlier. After each type of practice, you will likely decide to make some changes, either to the slides themselves or the way you talk about the material found there. You might even want to make notes within the presentation. Here we explain how to make notes in PowerPoint. Although we have chosen to offer details within this popular software, a notes feature is common to other programs as well.

When you are using PointPoint, below each slide is a section where you can jot down notes of what you would like to include in your talk when you present that slide. If your screen does not default to a screen with notes, click the Normal view icon circled below. In the following picture, do not worry about reading all the words; we just wanted to show you what the overall screen looks like.

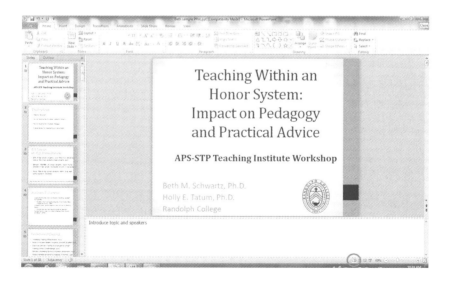

In the notes area, you can use full sentences or brief key points. Fewer words in the notes might help you focus better on key information and discourage you from reading aloud during your presentation. Before your talk, you can print out a copy of each slide with the notes below it. Under Print options, click Full Page Slides then Notes Pages.

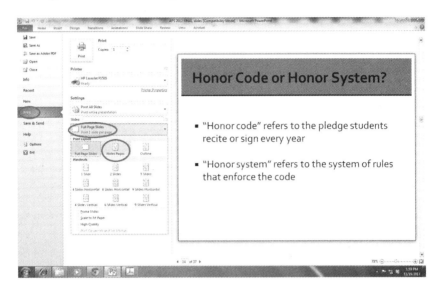

The slide is printed with the notes beneath. The words might be difficult to read here due to the page size, but we wanted you to see the full picture of what will be printed.

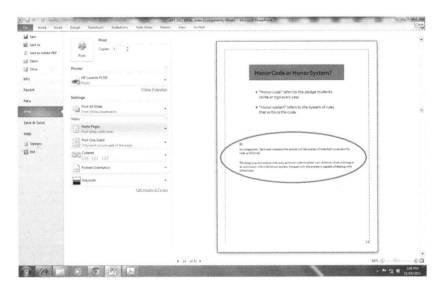

You will have plenty of space to write on the page after you print, adding any additional information you want to have in front of you when giving your presentation.

Reading (or *Not*) and the Pace of Your Talk

Even though we suggest the use of notes as reminders, we are not encouraging you to read them during your real-life presentation. And please do not read directly from your slides either. Absolutely not. That needs to be repeated. *Never read from your slides. Never, ever stand in front of an audience and read your slides.*

Other than having terrible (or no) slides, coming to the session drunk, or punching an audience member in the chin, reading from slides is the worst thing you can possibly do. Reading says you did not prepare well, you are too insecure to talk about your own work, or you think members of the audience lack intelligence. I assure you, the audience can read. The people in the room come to your presentation to see and hear a presentation. If they wanted to read slides, they could have e-mailed you for your paper and read it without paying good money to attend the conference.

To avoid reading, let us explore the main reasons why this might happen. Lack of preparation means you probably are not familiar enough with your slides to know what is on them. Or you have a vague idea of what they say, but you did not practice discussing them out loud. You should make sure that does not happen. Refer to the various forms of practice mentioned earlier.

Insecurity during a presentation can be tied to lack of practice, but what else? Perhaps you feel insecure because you do not have significant results. No matter. If you conducted a careful study or conducted an extensive review of the literature, you learned some piece of truth in the world. Or you learned how you might do things differently in a future study. Your audience is perfectly open to hearing that information. In fact, ending a talk with potential limitations and future directions, which is standard practice, focuses on what the future might hold.

You might instead feel insecure because you are nervous. Remember that even the most famous researchers feel anxious when giving a presentation. Standing in front of people means being evaluated, and evaluation makes nearly everyone nervous. If the fact that we all feel nervous does not make you feel better (it never made us feel better either), you might try imagining audience members in their underwear. That practice always seemed a bit odd to us, but hey, if it works . . . A third option of course is to relax as best you can (see Chapter 2) and get the job done.

Beyond the mistake of reading your slides, we have seen two other common mistakes: Having too little or too much material. The first mistake is the most difficult to fix while standing in front of an audience, so we will discuss too little material first.

When students get nervous (and they do), they tend to move quickly. Part of the problem is the desire to finish already and end the pain of standing before an audience. But another part is a lack of experience with pacing. Both of us have been teaching for many years, and we have learned how to watch students' faces during class, be aware of the passing of time, and create a comfortable pace for our audience. We certainly still make mistakes, but practice over a long period of time gives speakers an intuitive feel for acceptable pacing. You do not have years to gain intuition before your presentation, so we will offer other ways to fill your allotted time.

Let us say you have practiced your talk in a conference-like setting. You have adjusted your slides or ideas as you practiced, and maybe a practice audience gave you feedback during your talk. If the technology is available (e.g., a cell phone), you could record your talk to get a sense of how fast you are talking. Be sure to time your practice talk. Make sure you are right on target with the goal of a 12- to 13-minute presentation, leaving 2 to 3 minutes for questions. Then shave off about 5 minutes for the much faster pace you likely will use during the live presentation! Now we can make that presentation longer.

One way to lengthen your presentation is obviously to add more slides. You can easily add slides to your introduction because you had to cut it down when you summarized for the slides. It is always useful to provide relevant background information with past research that supports your hypotheses and ideas. You can also fairly easily add more information to your discussion section. In the discussion, you get to speculate about your results and offer your opinion, so you can simply offer more speculation and opinions. Adding to your method and results should not be an option because we assume you fully explained these two sections already. After all, these are the heart and soul of your project. However, you might add details of measures such as a scale to your method slides or sample questions from a survey used, and maybe you can add a graph to illustrate a secondary result. No matter where you choose to add slides, add them. And even though we suggest many places to add, the best place is the discussion at the end of your presentation because if you run out of time, you can just skip the ending slides altogether.

Another way to lengthen your talk is to have a handout. A handout should not be your presentation slides, although that is a standard practice at conferences. We prefer a handout designed specifically for the presentation. It might include a table with details that make it too difficult to read when projected. Or you might offer a copy of an important scale you used to assess a dependent variable. We recommend offering a handout while you are talking about your method or results because (1) the handout should help clarify what you are presenting, and (2) such a handout allows you to talk longer as you discuss key points. And for some reason, audience members appreciate handouts.

If you do choose to simply provide a paper copy of your presentation, you can distribute it before you begin your talk or at the end. If you feel you must offer such a handout, you should offer it at the end so people will focus on you during the presentation rather than read ahead and know your punch lines. Although a handout at the beginning allows people to take notes while you are talking, you must know that most will not take notes, and if they really want to write something down, they probably have a pen and paper. Again, please know that a handout of your slides will not offer new information and will not lengthen your talk in any way. And in today's digital world, it is very easy to send a copy of your presentation to anyone who asks for it. In fact, often people will ask for copies of your presentation. It is standard to agree to share your presentation with others. In Chapter 12 we include details on how and what to share with those who are interested in your research.

Remember that a second mistake is having too much material. If you are the type of student who talks slowly, talks a lot, or just meanders all over the place when talking, this section is for you. First, if you verbally wander, use your slides to keep you focused. If you talk slowly or use many words, practice your pacing until you are more comfortable with the material.

If you simply have too much material for the time you are given (for whatever reason), you must cut information. It is especially painful to cut from your slides because you already sweated over writing them. Those words came from you, and they seem like your children—almost. We understand. We feel the same way about papers we have written and then had to cut down to a specific size for a journal or remove entire sections that wandered off-topic. In fact, we generally feel better if we cut sections and paste them in a secondary file just in case we can use all of that hard work later. We rarely do, but saving the words makes us feel better at the time. Feel free to save your cut information to another file; go ahead and label the file *discard* when you name it.

You can also identify slides that could be cut if you are running over time. Just as people can lengthen their presentations with more slides, particularly at the end, you can cut slides, but focus on cutting from the end. Those cut slides could come in handy during the question-and-answer session. Someone could ask a question that pertains to information you had to cut due to time. Identify slides near the end of your presentation that you can skip or reserve for questions. Perhaps put a small symbol on them to remind you that the slide is not entirely needed for your presentation to make sense.

No matter how you remove information, do make sure you remove some. Do not waste time telling yourself that *all* of it is important, and do not reassure yourself that you really can cover all the information within 12 to 13 minutes. In such cases, the presenter ends up rushing through every single slide, and audience members do not have enough time to process the details. If you are still telling yourself that 50 slides can be covered, have you ever had a teacher who needed to cover a lot of information to cover in a class period (maybe the day before a test), so he or she raced through all the material? Do you remember how annoyed you were? You wanted the teacher to realize that a little less information would be okay. You wanted to see some understanding that poor planning on the part of the teacher should not translate into suffering for you. Yes, we have all experienced such a presentation, so avoid giving one.

Be Heard and Understood

At this point, you have read about what your slides should include and how to organize your talk for optimal communication about your research. Now we need to talk to you about some of the more subtle aspects of your presentation style that can really make a difference. We have both been in the audience of a presentation and had the person sitting next to us whisper, "I cannot hear a word she is saying," or "If he clears his throat one more time, I am going to scream!" That is exactly what we are going to help you avoid as you prepare for the day of your presentation.

Your talk is ready to go, you have a good idea of how long to stay on each slide, and you have practiced so much you can give the talk in your sleep (and maybe you have). Now, let us get to the nitty-gritty of *how* to speak so that everyone in the room can hear you and understand what you are saying. We assume some of you took a class on public speaking in which you covered some of the mechanics of voice and diction. But it never hurts to hear these tips more than once, especially when you are a little nervous about giving the talk. Even if you only have to give your talk to a professor or a classroom full of friends, simply knowing an audience exists is enough to instill some level of fear.

Although Chapter 2 offered some general strategies to overcome fear, we offer additional tips here. Try these approaches if you are nervous during your talk. Focus your attention on one friendly face in the middle of the audience. In fact, consider seating a friend or supportive colleague front and center, and focus on that person as needed. Although a little bit of stress can be beneficial, reducing some anxiety can be helpful when it comes to pacing your talk. Although you practiced many times, anxiety is likely to make you talk too fast.

In addition to increased speech rate, diction can suffer in front of an audience and with pressure to get the point across concisely. Just breathe. This advice might sound silly, and you might be thinking, "Of course I am going to breathe." But if you keep your breathing in the back of your mind (clearly your talk needs to be in the front of your mind) while you are talking, this can help you to slow your pace. You might have had the experience of simply talking so fast that you feel out of breath. If you find that happening during a presentation, it is a signal that you need to slow down. We admit that it is difficult to change a set pace, even if the pace is too fast. One solution is to have that friend or colleague in the audience ask a question in the middle of your talk. Listening to a question forces you to stop talking, think, and alter your rhythm to a more natural conversational pace. Some people are terrified to take a question during their talk for fear of losing their place in the presentation, but the benefits of better pacing and more interactive style outweigh the potential negative, at least for us.

During presentations, have you ever thought, "How many times is this person going to say 'um' during her talk?" We all have. Typically, fillers such as "um," "like," "okay," and "you know" are inserted when our mind has not yet determined the words we want to say, but we have already completed our previous points. What we like to tell our students is that you are better off with silence than any of these fillers. Though we know it is difficult to stand in front of an audience without any words coming out, do not fall into the trap of filling the silence with vocal junk. Using too many fillers creates the perception of a less polished presentation. And the silence that you think lasts forever is probably only a few seconds.

In addition to eliminating fillers and speaking at a rate that is understandable, you should consider the inflection of your voice for your talk. You might recall a teacher in your past who you considered a great cure for insomnia. Monotonous speaking, without any inflection or expression, often creates the impression that you are bored with your own presentation. If you model utter boredom, others will copy you. You want to sound passionate about your topic. You want to sound knowledgeable, interested, and confident during your talk. And to be honest, the sound of your voice strongly influences how you are viewed by those in the audience. By controlling your pace, breathing, inflection, and expression, you can significantly improve your ability to communicate the findings of your research. The way you talk can either make or break the connection you have with the audience.

Finally, listen to yourself as you talk. Keep your words simple. Give the information in a friendly conversational style. Do not desperately search for just the right big word or complex sentence structure. Too often we know students have stopped listening to what they are saying and have gone inside their own heads to search for impressive words or phrases. Stay in the moment, pay attention, and simply talk like a normal person.

Winning Over Your Audience

You can also significantly improve the connection you make with your audience by the amount of eye contact you make with them. You can start your talk by making eye contact with a familiar face to calm your nerves. But once your talk is underway, try to make eye contact with people in different sections of your audience. Make each person in that room feel that you are talking with him or her and want that person to really understand what you are saying.

After you learn to make eye contact, consider other ways to bond with your audience. For example, humor, if used correctly, can help connect you to the audience. Including humor can be helpful to get the audience's attention, keep the audience's attention, and communicate the take-home message of your presentation. A good rule of thumb is to include about two or three pieces of humor in a 15-minute talk. Including slides of cartoons can help get a laugh, but the cartoons should be relevant, readable from a distance, and not break up your pace in an artificial way. Avoid inside jokes that only a few audience members will understand and appreciate. If you decide to include humor, you need to be sure that what you say is actually funny and does not offend anyone in your audience. In terms of the question of offensive humor, our advice is that if there is any doubt, leave it out. Above all else, do not wait for laughter. Include your attempt at humor, hope that the audience understands it, assume the humor related well to your talk, and move on! Finally, if inserting humor makes you cringe, do not include it. When interacting with real people, be yourself. Be authentic.

When it comes to engaging your audience, you could consider including a question at the beginning of your presentation that gets everyone to really think about the topic at hand. Of course, this takes time away from your formal presentation, but the time can be well spent if you grab the audience members' attention from the start. As examples, you could start with asking attendees for their opinion; you could ask them for personal experiences that relate to the topic; or you could take a survey to see how many in the audience have had a particular experience that relates to your presentation. This connection to your audience right from the start is a great way to make sure everyone is paying attention to what you have to say.

In this chapter, we moved beyond the mechanics of building the visuals to accompany your oral presentation. We urge you to practice in many ways, incorporate feedback, and build in approaches to bond with your audience.

SECTION IV

Beyond Content

Putting Your Best Foot Forward

The Day *Before* Your Presentation 10

This is the part of the book where we give you very personal advice. We will go ahead and admit that right away. As you read our advice, please realize two things:

1. We have seen certain mistakes many, many times.

2. As professors, we know what professors think about those mistakes.

Your Travel Plans

Our advice actually begins even earlier than a day before your presentation. Our first suggestion is about traveling. Discuss travel to the conference with your professor. He or she will have ideas about the best way to get there and might even offer you a ride, if possible. If you travel by car, be sure the car is reliable. If you travel by mass transit, such as a plane, arrive at the airport early. Regardless of your method of travel, book early, and try to arrive at the conference the day before your presentation. Recall Murphy's Law: What can go wrong, will. Remember that time you waited until the last minute to print your paper for a class, and the printer did not work? You do not want a repeat of that nightmare. Arrive the day before, get to know the conference layout, and visit the room of your presentation. *Do not* make arrangements to travel the day of your presentation. You know as well as we do that flights can be cancelled, trains can be significantly delayed, cars can break down, or massive traffic can slow you down.

If your travel plans include family members, know that you will be busy at the conference. Sometimes we feel pulled between being with our family and attending conference sessions. Most conferences start at 8:00 in the morning and continue through the day until about 5:00 in the evening. You might be able to join your family for a lunch break, and indeed you might be free for an hour here or there, but your focus should be on the conference. Although we are not suggesting that you always travel alone, just understand that juggling work and family during a brief conference can be difficult. If the person who travels with you is an adult, know that some conferences allow you to register a companion at a small cost, which allows your guest to attend conference events.

You might be asking, why would my family want to come along? Just take a look at the locations of some of the conferences where you can present your work. Who would not want to join you in cities like Honolulu, Orlando, San Diego, Chicago, or Boston? Need we say more? These are great locations for conferences because of the large conference centers offered there. But the locations are also great for sightseeing, dining, and relaxing. When you attend conferences in these fabulous cities, you do need to recognize the need to attend the conference in general and not just give your presentation and then head to the amusement park or beach. This is particularly true when a granting agency or your home institution covers your travel expenses. There is an expectation that you are indeed traveling to attend the conference. To get around this dilemma, we typically add days at either end of the conference for sightseeing and personally pay for expenses during those additional days. Adding days is a good way to enjoy time with your travel companions *and* attend the conference as planned. During the conference, your time will be spent in sessions and talking with colleagues.

Professionalism at the Conference

Usually students congregate with other students at a conference. This can be a good thing. Hanging out with other students can help you commiserate about being nervous, discuss expectations from different professors, and tell fun stories related to research, instructors, and travel. You can also make lasting professional relationships with other students who are as motivated as you are. However, we have seen some definite downsides that we would like you to avoid. Allow us to tell you some stories.

Avoid Alcohol (and Other Mind-Altering Substances)

We have seen groups of students swim at the hotel pool well past midnight, play poker until 3:00 a.m., and drink alcohol the night before an 8:00 a.m. oral presentation. We have had students arrive at the conference the morning after partying, only to reek of alcohol, look terrible, and vomit into a ficus-tree planter.

Here let us remind you of some unfortunate after-effects of too much alcohol consumption:

Headache

Painful sensitivity to light and sound

Bloodshot eyes

Thirst

Fatigue

Restless sleep, if any

Dizziness

Nausea and probably vomiting

Rapid (or very slow) heartbeat

Shakiness

Depression, anxiety, irritability

Reduced ability to concentrate

If those symptoms fail to dissuade you from drinking, we can take a look at when you should get to the hospital or have a friend get you to a hospital:

Vomiting that will not stop

Seizures

Mental confusion, stupor, or losing consciousness

Slow or irregular breathing

Other than seizures, we admit that many hangovers include some of these symptoms, so you or your friends (or your professor) will have to be the judge of when to call 911. But no matter which symptoms seems particularly uncomfortable to you (we vote for the vomiting, but headache and feeling very tired are pretty awful too), none of them are useful at a professional conference. Not only will you feel terrible, but you will have to perform in some way during the day, and most people will know you suffer from a hangover—and bad judgment.

Nobody thinks these horrors will happen to them. But they will. And they do. And you can avoid embarrassing situations without too much work. When others want to have just one alcoholic drink, say no. Seriously, drink later. Do not drink at a conference. If it is the night before your presentation, drinking alcohol is just crazy. And even if you have already presented and merely plan to attend the conference the next day, avoid alcohol. You do not want your pores to exude alcohol when sitting near other attendees, and you certainly do not want to be in any way inebriated around other conference attendees who are out and about in the evenings. Consider yourself being interviewed and judged during your entire conference stay.

Sure, our advice so far may seem dire. What is the big deal? Why all the gloom and doom? So, we need to remind you of the two points earlier in this chapter.

1. We have seen certain mistakes many, many times.

2. As professors, we know what professors think about those mistakes.

And while we are lecturing about the evils of alcohol at a conference, let us take a minute to say the final night before returning home is not a good time to celebrate. You will have to get home. If that means a car ride, heaven help the people who are stuck in the car with you. And it will not be much better if you are alone, which means you have to drive while feeling sick. If you are traveling home by plane, we can assure you that the pilot is not concerned with the queasiness of your stomach. This flight will be the time the plane hits turbulence, and you will become familiar with those little white bags in the seat pocket in front of you. Please do not do this to yourself, and we beg you not to do this to the people who sit beside you. We have been those beside people, and one day you will be too. And while you are judging the person with the hangover, be thankful you do not feel that crappy. You will get off the plane and go on your merry way, enjoying memories of a great conference.

Get Plenty of Sleep

In addition to our advice of no alcohol, we strongly recommend getting a good night's sleep before your presentation. At least be in your hotel room resting quietly. The night before a presentation is not the time to stay up all night chatting with a friend or hotel roommate. Save late-night interactions for after your presentation, when you want to brag (but be humble) about how well your session went.

Even as we suggest getting a good night's sleep, we know you will be nervous. Being nervous makes your mind go over your fears many times, and that rumination can get in the way of sleep. Do your best. Try some relaxation exercises (Chapter 2). We also recommend warm milk, turkey, deep breathing, a boring book, or any other gentle remedy. We do not recommend sleep aids in the form of medication (unless your doctor already prescribed medication as part of ongoing treatment). Sleep medication can leave you dragging the next day, or worse, you might oversleep and miss your talk. Try the remedies offered in Chapter 2 to get the sleep you need. If you are a bit tired the next day, you can still give your talk in a professional manner.

Maybe lack of sleep is not a problem for you; perhaps you have trouble waking up. If you cannot seem to wake up well in the morning, you run the risk of missing your talk. Once again, know yourself. If waking up on time is a problem for you, make plans to solve your problem. Set an alarm and a back-up alarm, ask the hotel for a wake-up call, and ask a friend (or your instructor) to contact you at a certain time. You must get up in time to prepare for your talk, including dressing yourself well.

What to Wear

Over the years and conferences, we have noticed that students have a uniform. Men tend to wear khakis, a button-down shirt, and a blue blazer. Women tend to wear a black or brown suit with heels. Of course we have seen variations on those themes: Men sometimes add a tie or even wear a suit; women wear flat shoes with the black or brown suit. We see nothing wrong with the uniform, and in fact, students are making safe choices. Our only advice for change is for women to avoid high heels. Lately we have noticed an alarming trend toward higher shoes, and someone is going to get hurt. Our main complaint, however, is not tied to risk of injury—at least not physical injury.

Unless you are highly skilled at walking in high heels and can make it look natural, you just look silly maneuvering a conference when walking is such a chore. Bring the heels down a bit, make sure the suit fits correctly (especially not too tight), and send the message that you mean business. A conference generally requires a lot of walking, so make sure your shoes and clothes are comfortable but professional.

We probably do not even need to tell you to avoid jeans and T-shirts, but we will. Even jeans with a blazer fail unless you are a recognized expert in your field. Few people can pull this off at a traditional conference. If you take a chance with clothing at a conference, you will not be seen as quirky or adorable. Wear some version of the uniform and save risky styles for a different context. And save the jeans for evenings when you are exploring a new city.

Now that you know what to wear and what to avoid, give some thought to packing. If you must travel, clothing must travel well. Do not choose outfits that wrinkle easily. And to avoid that rumpled look, you might try the rolling technique when packing. Simply fold pants or a dress as much as is needed to, then roll the clothing up and avoid creases. Pack lightly if you can, and remember that a sweater or belt can entirely change the look of a simple dress. Men can get away with wearing the same outfit more than once, but consider wearing a fresh shirt on day two.

As a final packing tip, do not forget your poster or paper! You likely will not be able to recreate your work at the conference, and printing a large poster is extremely difficult when you are in a new and unfamiliar location where you probably have no transportation and are busy all day at the conference. Take the slides of your talk with you on a jump drive, e-mail a copy of the file to yourself, save the file to Dropbox, or print a copy and carry it with you. For a poster, we suggest purchasing a mailing tube of the correct length and storing your poster. Put the tube right on top of your suitcase or beside the door like a hospital bag packed for the night a woman goes into labor. Put sticky notes all over your room to remind you of the poster. After all, your presentation is the reason you are traveling, so do not forget it while focusing on what to wear and how excited you might be.

Although we mainly focus on conferences, all the same advice holds true for class presentations or any professional presentations. Err on the side of too professional—taking a presentation too seriously. Even if other people tease you about being dressed up or having too many back-up locations for your files, they will secretly envy you, especially when your high work ethic earns you a satisfying career.

The Day *of* Your Presentation 11

We will go ahead and assume that you had a solid 8 hours of sleep and woke up bright and early on the day of your presentation. Most likely, you will either give your talk first thing in the morning, or you will attend talks and poster sessions offered by other participants. You definitely want to stay involved and make the most of your conference experience. Do not be intimidated by the idea of attending a conference with experts in the field. Instead, take advantage of this wonderful learning opportunity. Look at the conference program, and choose the presentations that seem interesting to you. Talk with people, make contacts, and in general make yourself feel more comfortable with the atmosphere. Increased comfort in this context will reduce anxiety when presenting your own work.

As the time for your presentation approaches, arrive at least 10 minutes early. If your talk is later in the day and you want to take a quick peek at the room where you will be presenting, by all means find the room. A forewarning: At larger conferences the convention centers can be mazelike. So finding the location will also let you know how much time will be needed to get to the room later. And just seeing the room can often reduce the anxiety of the unknown.

If you are presenting a poster, many conferences allow you to put up your poster well before the presentation time. Be sure to find out how soon you can hang up your poster. Then come back 10 minutes early for the actual poster session. For a talk, you might be tempted to arrive very early, but usually other presentations are booked in the room throughout the day, and conference organizers offer about 10 minutes between sessions for setup of the next session as well as time for the current session to shut down and address any lingering questions.

In this chapter, we briefly discuss how to put your best foot forward during your presentation, beginning with posters and ending with paper presentations. Remember that prior chapters in this book offer more detailed information on how to create different types of presentations.

Poster Etiquette

On the day of your presentation, know when posters can be set up and arrive at the poster-session room at that time. Most likely you will see a large room filled with rows of free-standing cork bulletin boards that are 4×8 feet. The exact size should have been communicated to you in your e-mail acceptance note. With two sides on each board, presenters often are expected to fit two posters on each side for a total of four posters per bulletin board. Not all conferences will have this standard setup; conference organizers should offer details before you arrive. If not, e-mail them and ask prior to printing your poster.

You will notice that each poster spot is labeled with a number, and you should have been given a number associated with your poster. When you arrive, locate your poster spot to see if you have a good spot or a bad spot. A good spot allows a lot of participant traffic, usually near one of the entry doors. A bad spot is way off in a back corner somewhere and maybe even on the side of the board that faces the back wall. Not to worry, people will still visit your poster, but higher traffic areas are best. This said, if your conference does not specify a location, arrive early and pick a good spot.

When you think about presenting your poster, it might be tempting to decide you will feel less stress if only a few people stop by. Nothing could be further from the truth (for most people). Imagine how uncomfortable you would feel if you had to stand in front of a poster alone with a vacant smile on your face for an entire hour. All around you, other people are chatting with attendees about their research, smiling, laughing, networking, and maybe even planning to conduct research together. These awkward moments happen to most presenters at some point. To avoid feeling like an outsider, keep your body language open and take every opportunity to welcome people.

Now that you are standing in front of your spot, how do you get the poster on the board? Many conference organizers will offer pushpins (tacks) to put up your poster. As another option, you could borrow some pins from the person next to you who planned ahead. Of course you know we suggest that you be that plan-ahead person and let people borrow from *you*. Most likely you will need only six to eight pushpins to secure your poster to the board. After that is done, and you have been careful to stay within your allotted space on the board, you can relax until the official start time. Well, you can relax until 10 minutes before the start time because you want to be early. You might even consider roaming around and looking at the other posters while authors set up. Often this time will be your only opportunity to talk with other presenters.

When the poster session begins, you will be asked to stand with your poster for about one hour. Some sessions require two hours, but one hour is standard. Occasionally, a hotel or convention center will place a chair or two beside each board. We urge you to stand the entire time. In fact, we suggest removing the chair from your area and placing it by the wall, if you can, to avoid the temptation of sitting. No poster presenter should sit during a session unless there is a physical reason to sit. Otherwise, remain standing to welcome visitors.

In fact, your body language can make or break a poster presentation. Stand a bit to the side of your poster, turn your body outward to welcome visitors, and smile with eye contact as often as possible. As you read the body language of approaching (or wandering) attendees, look for signs that they are willing to learn about your project. Tips include willingness to make eye contact, pausing ever-so-slightly in front of your poster, reading the title or any other part of your poster, and even glancing at the number of your poster and matching it to paperwork in their hands (usually a conference program or listing of posters). Take any of these opportunities to say, "Hello, can I tell you about my research?" Or you might offer, "Hi, can I give you an overview of my study?" Or even, "Would you like a handout?"

If you hit a lull in the stream of participants, consider getting to know the people presenting near you. Ask about their research, how well they like the conference, and which talks they have attended. If you invite people to share their research with you, hopefully they will reciprocate and ask you to do the same. But we offer two cautions: (1) Excuse yourself from the conversation if an attendee stands in front of your poster and starts reading or otherwise expresses an interest in talking with you, and (2) do not wander away from your own poster. Likewise, if you are talking with another presenter, and an attendee walks up to his or her poster, excuse yourself from the conversation in recognition that you can chat later when no one is waiting.

Now imagine that someone walks up and, without a word, begins to read your poster. Never stand by while visitors read. You are there to share. Always offer, "Can I summarize the poster for you?" You might even say, "I know it's a lot to read. Can I tell you about the study?" People almost always say yes, and they appreciate the personal interaction. Give a general overview of what you studied and how, ending with your results and potential explanations. Be brief; come prepared with a 2- to 3-minute summary of your research. Usually participants will ask follow-up questions or even give advice. Be sure to accept criticism graciously, saying something like, "That's interesting. I'll look into that," or "Oh, I hadn't realized that. What's the name of the author who does that research? I'll look it up when I get back home." Never ever say, "Well that's annoying. I worked really hard on this, and you should be supportive," or "You're not the smartest person I've ever met, and I think I know more about my own study than you do!" And of course never stick out your tongue, frown (unless in serious concentration), or stomp your foot. You get the idea. Be gracious, be professional, be kind, and be welcoming.

While people are stopping at your poster and learning about your research, you will notice that attendees are young, old, informal, formal, or any other variations you can imagine. Do not assume that a younger informal visitor is a student. Do not put aside your professional demeanor in favor of student bonding. You will not know for sure the background or educational level of the person in front of you, so remain professional at all times. If you would like to use the person's name while talking, glance at his or her name tag and opt for "Doctor" and the person's last name. If you are wrong, the attendee will correct you. Do not try to glean more about the visitor by staring at a name tag because that just gets weird.

We already covered the need for a one-page handout of your poster in Chapter 3, but let us reiterate here. People often will want a handout. We anticipate changes in the future, with people simply scanning a Quick Response (QR) code on your poster, allowing them to locate your information later. But we are not there yet. For now, bring plenty of handouts. We recommend 25 as a minimum, and you should also have available a piece of paper for people to write down their e-mail address in case you need to send them a copy after the conference. Please note that many people will stop by just for a handout and not to read your poster. They will read your handout later. But as often as possible, use their quick visit as an opportunity to summarize your poster. Do not be offended if attendees simply want the handout. There are many posters in one session, and those attending must choose which posters they have time to visit.

Oral-Presentation Etiquette

You already know to arrive 10 minutes early, and you know that a prior session probably will be wrapping up (recall more information on preparations in Chapter 9). If the schedule says the prior session ends at 2:50, arrive at 2:50, but know that the speakers might be going a bit over on time. Sure, it is not fair, but it happens. Your job is to be kind and respectful anyway. Stand in the back of the room or, if the doors are up front, quietly find the nearest place to sit in the audience and wait. When the time is 2:55, you can subtly wave and smile at the presenter or moderator. If possible, you can quietly tap the moderator on the shoulder and ask if you can set up. You will need five minutes to plug in your computer and get your PowerPoint ready to go before your scheduled starting time.

For a slightly different scenario, you might arrive at 2:50 and see that the official talk is over, but people are milling around up front, chatting with the speakers. It is fine to smile, say hello, and ask if you can set up. If the presenter is clearly in a conversation, you can begin to set up anyway, being careful not to move the presenter's materials without asking first.

Usually the room is set up in a specific way for talks. Talks are also called *symposia* or *paper sessions*. A symposium generally refers to a group of several oral presentations in one hour submitted together as a group. Sometimes a symposium only has one speaker, but a single speaker in an entire hour is a bit less likely. A paper session is a group of brief talks grouped together by conference organizers based on similar topics. You will most likely present your work in a paper session. The room should have a podium up front, a white projection screen, and a projector. You might also notice a table up front by the podium and a few chairs behind it. This table is set up for presenters to face the audience until it is their turn at the podium. Of course the audience will have chairs set up in theater style, but occasionally they might sit at tables. You need to bring a laptop because most conferences do not provide one. If you have a Mac computer, plan to bring an adaptor because many projectors come with connectors only for a PC.

A moderator should be waiting to greet you. When you walk up front with your computer and notes, it will be obvious that you are one of the speakers. Look for others up front who might also be speakers; introduce yourself, and ask if they are presenting. If the order of speakers has not been decided, you can discuss that with the other speakers (and moderator). Please note that the order of papers almost always goes in the order they appear in the conference program. The first person listed should go ahead and set up the computer. Symposium presenters might decide to put all presentations on one computer and minimize them on the screen. This set-up will make transitions between speakers go quickly and allow full presentation time for each person. We should note here that most conferences employ computer specialists who can troubleshoot if you have problems. If needed, ask the moderator to locate help.

The moderator should ask you how you want to stay on time. He or she can verbally tell you when you have 5 minutes left, then 2 minutes left, then time is up (or whatever time points you choose). Most moderators prefer to hold up fingers to indicate number of minutes left because it is less disruptive than talking. Finally, some moderators will come prepared with slips of paper with numbers on them to hold up when time is nearly up. If you do not have a moderator, keep close track of time, or ask another presenter to let you know when you have about 3 minutes left to wrap up.

When it is time to begin the session, a moderator should welcome attendees and briefly introduce each speaker by name and maybe title of the paper. When your turn comes, note the time and maybe put a cell phone (in silent mode) on the podium to show you a clock, and make sure your title slide is displayed on the white screen. Straighten your posture, make eye contact with your audience as much as possible, and smile from time to time or at least at the beginning and end of your talk. Remember that your goal is to share your work in a professional presentation. Be aware of nonverbal behaviors that communicate you are competent and kind. Competence will help people believe what you are telling them about your research, and kindness will make people want to learn from you. A kind, competent demeanor also goes a long way toward creating a supportive audience full of people who might ask you questions at the end of your presentation. You want to be friendly to these people!

Verbal behaviors come into play too. We discuss using your voice well in Chapter 9, with ways to be most effective in your speech style during your presentation as well as what to avoid.

- Do not tell the audience you are nervous. That admission makes people uncomfortable, and you are still expected to be competent. (See Chapter 2.)
- Do not try to wow your audience with big words and complex sentences. Keep it simple and focus on sharing with your audience. If you are constantly searching for the next impressive word or phrase, you will not even hear your own speech! Listen to yourself as you talk. Be in the moment. When you stop worrying about impressing people and focus only on communication, the presentation will go much more smoothly.
- Avoid lots of "ums" and "ahs" and throat clearings. These distancers indicate that the speaker is looking for the perfect word or sentence structure. Refer to the prior point.
- Do *not* read from the slides. Nothing could be more tedious. Use the slides as a trigger for your memory, and then tell your story while looking at the audience as much as possible.

Your computer will be at the podium, so many speakers choose to present from the podium. This location is perfectly acceptable; however, you may want to step from behind the podium occasionally and even walk across the front of the room. Try not to pace rapidly, block the screen, or saunter in a pompous manner. If you are wearing those high heels we warned you about, stay behind the podium. Walking increases the probability of wobbling or tripping, and it is difficult to sell professionalism on unsteady feet. It is even worse to end up sprawled on the floor.

During your presentation, an audience member might leave the room. As long as the attendee leaves quietly, try not to be offended. Stepping out of a session is acceptable and could mean the person realized he or she was in the wrong session, had to go to the bathroom, needed a drink of water, or made the mistake of drinking alcohol the night before. Another reason a person leaves a session is that he or she really wants to hear the first presentation but needs to get to another session to hear the third presentation there. It is for this reason the moderator will try to keep speakers in the order of the program and on time. Again, do not take it personally. In fact, in addition to people leaving the room in the midst of the session, you will see people entering the room as well.

While you are talking, an audience member might raise his or her hand or simply speak out a question. Do not be concerned that you have lost your rhythm. A question from the audience often allows speakers to see from the audience's perspective and helps them communicate more clearly. A question lets you take a deep breath and unwind (remember our advice in Chapter 9).

Most likely, the moderator will ask for questions at the end of your talk. Be sure to leave at least 2 minutes for questions to avoid going over your allotted time. You can have three types of questions: dumb, intelligent, and narcissistic.

The first two are handled the same way: Politely answer both dumb and intelligent questions. If you are not sure of what is being asked, kindly request for clarification, or rephrase the question, and ask if your paraphrase is a correct interpretation, then answer it when you have a clear understanding. You do not have to be an expert. If you are unsure of an answer, simply say that you are unsure. Maybe even ask the attendee what he or she thinks or suggests for further reading in the area.

The narcissistic question (or questioner) is the toughest to handle. This person is rude or clueless or both. He or she could be anyone in the audience. A narcissistic question is easy to spot. It is usually the longest, most meandering, hypothetical, or philosophical question imaginable. For example, "You have looked at the influence of companionship on quality of life, but have you considered reviewing your results in terms of a theory tied to the evolutionary underpinnings of survival of a species across time?" Because a narcissistic question often cannot be answered, we focus on how to respond gracefully.

One option is to offer ego support. "No, I hadn't thought of this from an evolutionary perspective. That's an interesting approach. Let me give it some thought. If you'll be around later, I'd like to get your ideas." Usually this response removes your problem. You have recognized the question as valid, and you have offered to continue the discussion later. It is highly unlikely that the attendee will want to discuss it later, but you have offered. In fact, offering to talk later during the conference or follow-up with electronic communication is a good approach to any question that monopolizes time.

A second option is to ask the moderator for clarification. This approach puts the burden on someone more experienced than you. Besides, the moderator is probably looking for a way to save you and will welcome the opportunity to step in. Sometimes the moderator can rephrase the question for you, say you are out of time, or suggest that the questioner contact you after the session. Under no circumstances should a moderator leave you standing there feeling uncomfortable, but if that happens, try the ego-support option above.

So far we have focused on the types of questions you may get, but we need to remind you that speakers have etiquette rules to follow too. When you answer a question, be concise. Do not ramble on. If possible, return to a figure or table in your slideshow that helps support your answer. Make eye contact and maintain a friendly facial expression. Continue to be kind and competent.

When you have finished answering questions, or time is up, thank the audience. Ending can feel awkward, so we suggest planning how you will wrap up your talk. A good ending is to say, "I would like to thank my instructor for helping me with this research, and thank you for your time." Keep it simple, do not keep talking, and smile before you turn to sit down. Sometimes the audience will clap, sometimes not, it depends on the climate of the session. If the moderator wants clapping at the end of each individual talk, he or she will likely begin it after you have said, "Thank you" and made a move to leave the podium. It is almost certain that the audience will clap at the end of the entire session because this is standard conference practice.

After all talks in your session are finished, the moderator will thank the audience for attending. Most attendees will leave. But you can bet that some people will come to the front to tell you what a great job you did, ask you a question, or just introduce themselves to you. This is the part of the presentation when you smile, shake hands, nod, collect e-mail addresses for later contact, and make people glad they came up front to make a personal connection with you. However, keep in mind that the next session will soon begin. Try to pack up while still making the final guests feel welcome. Move them toward the door with your body language, and if necessary, ask them to step outside with you to chat.

It is finally time to walk away from the talk with a smile on your face. If the conference is ongoing, continue to attend sessions and meet people. You might even see people who attended your session, and it is very possible that people will continue to let you know how much they enjoyed your presentation.

The Day *After* Your Presentation 12

It is time to go home, and if you presented a poster, you are probably wondering what to do with it now. Yes, you should definitely bring it back with you. You worked far too hard on your presentation to leave your work behind. Think of the space you could fill on the wall over your couch or over your bed. Seriously, you can proudly display it at home, or your teacher might want to put it in his or her lab or office space. Or perhaps your teacher's department at school may want to display conference posters and show off their students' hard work. As another possibility, you might have the opportunity to display your poster at an on-campus function that highlights student research.

The examples offered above are ways to display accomplished work, but notice that we are not suggesting you use the same poster at another conference. Although small on-campus functions are generally acceptable second venues, you should only present your work at a single outside conference. In fact, most conferences remind you of this restriction on their website or submission paperwork. Conference organizers want to include original work in the program and not work already presented elsewhere.

Contacts and Good Manners

When you return home from the conference, follow up on contacts you made there. Within a day or two, look over any notes that you made about who talked with you at your poster session or your talk. While the experience is still fresh in your mind, contact those who had questions or wanted a copy of your presentation. If you are lucky, someone may even have wanted to collaborate with you on a research project. Or maybe someone recruited you for graduate school. A brief but friendly e-mail is appropriate. Consider your audience when deciding the tone of your e-mail, and err on the side of too formal. If the recipient is a professor, be sure to use "Dr." in the greeting, followed by his or her last name. If the recipient is another student, you could use his or her first name and no title.

Conference attendees may have asked for a copy of your poster (if you ran out of copies or they want it in digital form), a copy of your paper, or even your PowerPoint slides. All of these requests are fairly standard, and most presenters will honor such requests. In fact, you may ask presenters for these materials too, but be sure to tell them (1) you want to learn more about their work, and (2) you will give them credit if you show someone a slide from their presentation.

Although researchers tend to share their work with others, we do not usually share our data sets. First, data sets are personal, so their setup is for our eyes only and make sense to us (e.g., column headings). Second, sharing data is questionable from an ethical standpoint because these are confidential data from participants. Lack of names does not guarantee confidentiality. Third, and we hope no one would actually do this, someone could analyze your data and publish results. We doubt that this unscrupulous behavior would occur, but the first and second reasons are good enough to avoid e-mailing data to a random conference participant. Of course, if you plan to collaborate with someone you met at the conference, you both can decide how to proceed with sharing data.

Whether you share your poster, manuscript, or PowerPoint slides, or merely send a polite follow-up email, make sure the e-mail has your name and contact information at the bottom. This is often called a signature file and can be set up in e-mail programs as an automatic add-on to outgoing messages. Yes, your e-mail address is part of your message, but a full name and contact information are helpful.

The following are some examples. The first one would be appropriate when contacting a professor.

Dear Dr. Schwartz,

We met briefly at the American Psychological Association conference, where I presented a poster of my research on rapport in teaching. I enjoyed talking with you and appreciated your suggestions for future research. You also requested a copy of my paper, which I have attached to this e-mail. Please let me know if I can offer more information.

Sincerely,

Janie Wilson

As an alternative, the e-mail on the next page would be reasonable when contacting a student.

> Dear Jennifer,
>
> We met at the recent APA convention in DC, where I presented a talk on an ego-depletion study. After the talk, you mentioned that you would like to consider collaborating. I've attached my paper to give you more details on my recent study. Feel free to e-mail me if you would like to brainstorm a follow-up project or if you have one of your own in mind.
>
> Take care,
>
> Janie

If you spoke with someone about the possibility of graduate school, you will also want to offer a follow-up e-mail.

> Dr. Wilson,
>
> We met last weekend at the Association for Psychological Science conference, where I presented a talk on information avoidance. At that time, you suggested that I apply to your university's PhD program in experimental psychology. I am very interested in learning more about your program and would appreciate guidance on how to present a strong application. In particular, I would like to work in your lab and continue the line of research we discussed. Thank you in advance for any information you have time to offer.
>
> Sincerely,
>
> William Gordon

Notice that the notes are indeed brief. Most people do not want to get a long e-mail that seems overwhelming. And of course the notes should, as much as possible, communicate a friendly and humble attitude. We do not suggest emoticons in professional e-mails, so sometimes communicating a friendly tone is tough. We hope our examples help as you draft your own postpresentation e-mails.

Will people respond? Not always. Often people return to the business of everyday life and put a conference behind them immediately. Discarding conference activities is common and does not reflect a lack of interest in the material. Life returns to normal, and other demands take precedence. The important point is that you should not allow busy life to interfere with personal e-mail contacts after your presentation. In fact, we have been impressed by speakers who responded to our interest in their work within a few hours, even while the conference is ongoing! The bottom line: Be professional by following up with interested colleagues, and do so within a few days of your presentation.

On the same note as connecting with colleagues, be sure to thank your instructor for any help and encouragement you received. Most likely, your work really was a joint effort between the two of you, and teachers rarely receive thanks from their students. A lot of thought and behind-the-scenes work went into preparing the course you took, thinking about your research, and reviewing your research efforts. Even if you think your instructor could have been more helpful or encouraging, you should offer thanks.

Because you see your instructor at school, you can offer a heartfelt thank you in person. However, an e-mail is also acceptable.

Dear Dr. Schwartz,

Thank you for helping me with my research project and encouraging me to attend the recent APS conference. I enjoyed conducting the research and learned a lot about the process. Attending the conference also taught me about professional presentations, and now I understand what to expect when presenting my work. Once again, thank you for your support of students.

Sincerely,

Maggie Valley

We have even received handwritten thank-you notes from students, and we appreciate the effort they took to write and give us a note. We both prefer an e-mail or electronic letter that could be included in annual-review reports to administrators, but any kind of thank-you note certainly is appreciated. Finally, we have received gifts from students. As long as the gifts are small, this practice might be okay. We have received homemade cookies, stuffed animals, chocolate milk powder, and a book relevant to the research area. Receiving gifts sometimes feels a bit awkward, but again, the thought of thanks is kind and appreciated.

One final contact issue to consider is the e-mail address you use. Hopefully you have a professional e-mail through your institution. But whether you do or not, make sure your e-mail address will not embarrass you. Keep it simple and conservative. As an extension, if you are available on Facebook, be sure you keep your pictures private, especially if you are shown drinking and partying in many of them. People who want to know you better—perhaps before they offer you a spot in their graduate program—will sometimes look up information about you on the web. If an instructor or student at a conference suggests a Facebook follow-up, we will leave that up to you. In general, most instructors view Facebook as a social network, although people are beginning to use it as a professional network as well. If you will use it professionally, we suggest creating a separate Facebook account for professional contacts.

The Paperwork

A last wrap-up activity you might need to do is complete paperwork for reimbursement. If your department or school, a grant agency, or even your teacher is helping to cover the cost of your conference attendance, expense receipts are needed. Be organized, and offer receipts for everything, including (if relevant) the following items:

- Airfare receipt (printed from your computer is fine)
- Checked-luggage receipt from the airline
- Boarding passes
- Food, including an itemized list and the tip amount on the receipt
- Parking costs (e.g., airport)
- Cab or shuttle fares, including the tip on the receipt
- An original receipt from the hotel marked with a zero balance
- Miles driven in your car and gas receipts
- Receipt for conference registration

Now What?

You conducted research, whether empirical or a literature review, wrote up your work in some format, presented your research in a professional manner, and followed up on contacts as needed. You should feel proud of yourself!

In the final two chapters of this book, we detail how to share your hard work in two additional ways: archiving video and publishing. A video of your oral presentation can be made available to many audiences, and viewers may choose to watch the video at their convenience. Although few conferences now video their presentations, you might use this technology to share your talk with a teacher or classmates as well. In Chapter 13 we will focus on how you might create your own video for later viewing.

A second way to share your research more broadly is publication. If you think your work is of the quality and outcomes you might see in a journal, talk with your instructor about the possibility of submitting a manuscript for publication. Your instructor should be honest with you and tell you whether or not the work is potentially publishable. Qualities of a publishable paper include:

- An original research question or idea
- A thorough review of relevant literature
- A solid methodology
- Approval from the institutional review board to conduct your study
- Interesting, significant results
- Clear, concise writing with no errors

If your teacher agrees that you should submit your paper to a journal, take a look at Chapter 14 for the steps-by-step instructions. And good luck!

Regardless of whether you submit your paper to a journal, you have already taken a big step in your professional development by presenting your research in some way. Sharing our work with each other is a crucial part of the research community. If your presentation was limited to the classroom or a small on-campus event, consider presenting at a conference. And welcome to the community!

SECTION V

Sharing With a Wider Audience

Video Yourself 13

Asynchronous Presentations

The poster and paper presentations we discussed in prior chapters are synchronous. In other words, the classroom or conference presentations happen in front of a live audience. In addition to the traditional type of live presentation, you might find the need to record your presentation for later viewing.

What Are Your Options?

As teachers, we sometimes find ourselves with large classes that make it difficult to include student presentations during class time. However, we want our students to have the valuable opportunity to present their work, and we want students in the class to learn from each other. In these situations, we turn to recording. If an instructor has not yet asked you to present your work as a recording, such a request is likely to happen with larger class sizes. Or you might want to record your presentation for another purpose such as applying for an award or scholarship. Regardless of why you need a sharable format, we want you to be ready.

As a presenter, you have to decide what kind of presentation you will offer. You can prepare a video of yourself in an empty classroom, projecting your visual information (such as PowerPoint slides) on a screen behind you. If you can arrange to have people in the room to serve as audience members, a live audience might be an option. As an alternative to recording a video of yourself standing in front of a classroom, you might simply show your visual materials, allowing each component to fill the screen, in which case you are heard but not seen. For example, perhaps you would like to show each slide of a PowerPoint presentation and allow only an audio of your voice discussing each slide. Of course you might also show yourself talking from time to time just to add a more personal touch. Regardless of the final format you choose, we recommend that your presentation contain both an audio and a visual component.

After the video file is created (details are below), you need to share it in some way. Before improvements in technology, we asked students to put their video on a CD and hand the disk to us. Rarely would e-mail attachments come through because files were too large. More recently, we have requested recorded presentations from students via uploading to YouTube, where a private link can be shared to locate a video. We have also taken advantage of Dropbox, asking students to upload brief videos and to share the link with us. For YouTube and Dropbox options, students can also share a link with other students in the class, allowing an entire class community to view presentations. Other options are available, and we know additional outlets will come along at a fast pace.

In this chapter, we describe several ways to create your presentation when you must record it for later viewing. Let us begin with standing in front of a classroom.

Old School: Get Out the Camera

You can go old school by finding an empty classroom and simply recording your presentation. We do not suggest recording in your living room with other people running around, although one of us has recorded a lecture in her home while on maternity leave. Unfortunately, a two-year-old big brother interrupted the lecture by racing past the camera naked. Also unfortunately, the recording was primitive, when such an interruption meant completely redoing the entire lecture. Needless to say, the naked child stayed in the recording, and no more lectures were recorded from home.

If you have identified a professional location with a white screen for projection, set up your camera on a sturdy tripod. Having someone hold the camera and record you means nausea for those who view the video later. Decide whether or not you want other people in the room. If you want an audience just to make the room look more interesting, invite some quiet friends who do not fidget and are willing to wear professional clothing. But know that zooming out to show an audience takes attention away from you and your slides. In fact, zooming out too far obscures slides so much that they are not readable. If, on the other hand, you want audience members to ask questions during or after your presentation, be sure to tell them exactly what they should ask. We recommend not inviting audience members to your talk unless you have a good reason. However, we also recognize that you may be entirely capable of making a high-quality video and incorporating an audience well.

When you are setting up the camera, check the screenshot to make sure your visual aids are clear. Zoom in as much as possible while keeping yourself in the picture. Check the lighting. If it is too bright in the room, your slides will not show up, but if it is too dark in the room, you will not be visible. Try to find a happy medium with lighting, zoom in, and take a practice video or still shot to make sure the video will be clear. A practice shot will also ensure good focus and show you any potential problems. If everything looks clear, and both you and your slides are visible, take a quick practice video to check the audio. Often, a camera has a microphone on it, but remember that the camera is now across the room and may not pick up your voice well. If you notice a problem, try to speak louder, and bring the camera as close as you can while maintaining good video coverage. After testing, you are ready to do your presentation.

It should go without saying that you have excellent visual aids (such as a Prezi), have practiced several times, and are wearing professional clothing (see prior chapters for advice). Take a few deep breaths and begin. You will be tempted to interrupt yourself and start over many times. For some reason, people get nervous as soon as a camera is turned on, even when a real person is not in the room watching. Maybe this is true because we think of the camera as a person, or we are imagining the people who will watch the video later. Either way, try to push through an entire presentation as soon as you begin. Otherwise, you can second-guess every sentence and take hours to record a 12-minute video. Keep in mind that you can easily alter a digital recording by recording sections of your lecture again and pasting the new pieces in as needed. As long as you have not procrastinated, you will have plenty of time to improve the recording after you run through the entire presentation.

Now that we have explained how to record yourself in a classroom and what potential problems to avoid, we must admit that this simple approach is not very sophisticated. The lighting and audio rarely produce a clear presentation, and usually the camera angle does not include both the speaker and slides well. As an alternative, you could consider showing your slides and adding only your voice discussing the slides.

Talking Slides: Voiceover PowerPoint

First, collect necessary hardware: a computer with audio input, which may require purchasing an external microphone. We have used a headset with a microphone to speak without awkwardly leaning forward to talk into a microphone on the desk. Other than presentation software that allows audio input, the external microphone is all you need.

Begin with your prepared PowerPoint presentation (we are using version 2010). Open the presentation, and choose the Slide Show tab at the top of your screen.

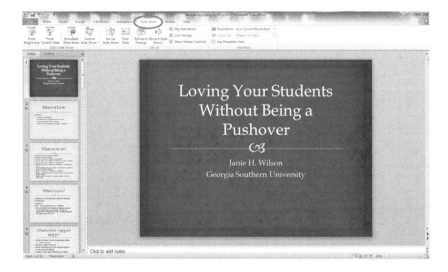

Click on the icon labeled Record Slide Show. Then you can choose to either start recording on the first slide of your presentation or record only on the current slide (which just happens to be the first slide in our example). You get to decide which slides contain audio and the details of the audio.

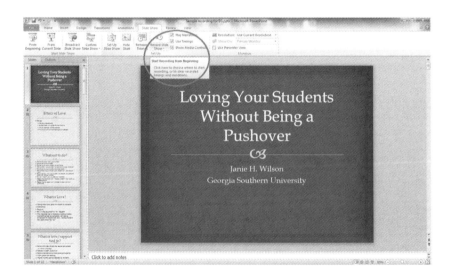

We clicked Start Recording from Beginning, and the small box in the next screenshot opened in the middle of the screen.

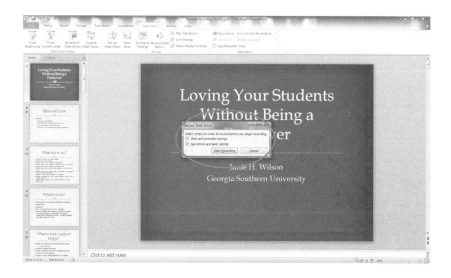

We left the default settings and clicked Start Recording. Notice that the slide fills the screen, and a small audio timer appears in the upper left corner.

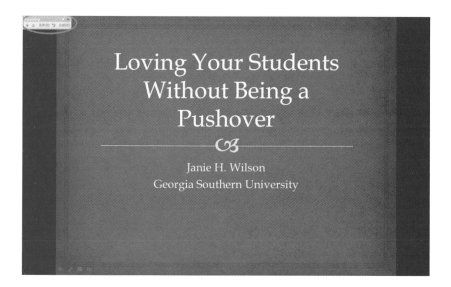

The timer (the one in the middle of the small box) is already advancing, so be ready to record right away. If you want to pause, simply click the pause button, which is the second icon from the left. As you speak, use the mouse or advance arrow buttons on your keyboard to bring in new elements of your slide if you have created a presentation with bullets coming in at separate times. Be careful to touch the mouse or keys gently so they are not picked up in the audio; this clicking can be distracting to the listener. If you are not happy with what you record, click the icon between the two timers to erase and record again. When you have finished recording audio for the specific slide, you can click the X button to stop recording and return to the PowerPoint presentation. Notice in the next screenshot that the slide now has a speaker icon on the bottom right to indicate that the slide contains an audio portion.

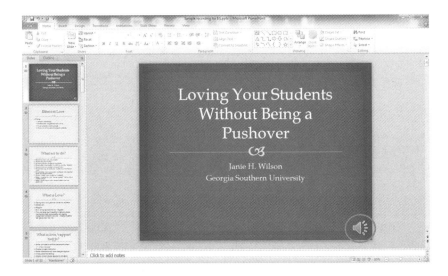

If you want to hear the audio in this view, put the cursor over the speaker icon to reveal a bar to play audio.

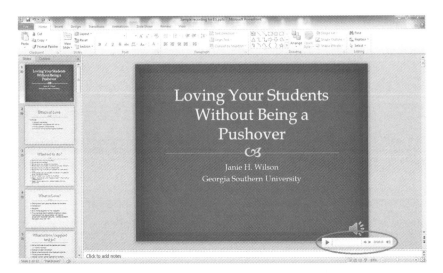

If you do not like what you hear, click on the icon to select it, then delete to remove audio from the slide. Or right click after selecting the icon to open a menu with many options. Here you can choose Delete, alter the audio by selecting a specific segment, or reformat the speaker icon.

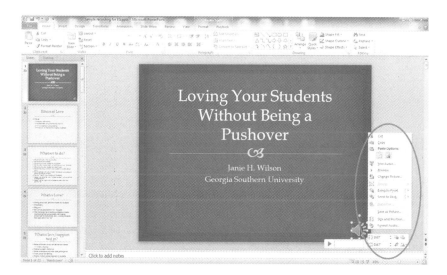

If instead of exiting the recording screen on the first slide, you had wanted to keep recording through several slides, you could have clicked the Next icon (a forward arrow on the left side of the small box) to move to the next slide while still recording. Notice that the middle timer begins at zero again for the second slide, but the timer to the right provides a cumulative time. Total time of your audio is extremely useful because you probably have a time limit for your entire presentation.

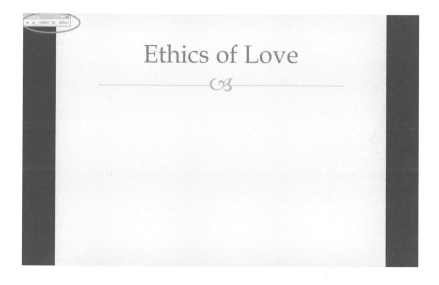

When you have recorded on the second slide (and as many additional slides as you would like), click the X button at the top right of the small window to return to your entire presentation. Notice that the speaker icon now appears on the first two slides—the ones on which you recorded audio.

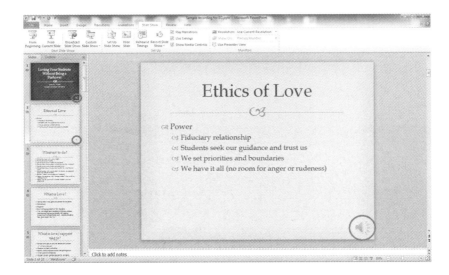

After you have recorded as much as you want to say, the length of audio will be at the bottom left of each slide.

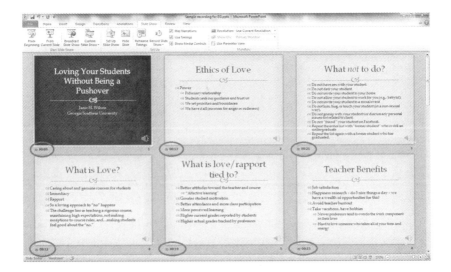

At this point, you might be thinking that you have to do more work to have a complete presentation with correct timings for each slide. But not to worry, recording audio while introducing new bullets and advancing slides already put the correct times on your slides. Your presentation should play smoothly. Watch it from the beginning with a critical eye, and decide if any particular slide needs new audio. When it is as good as you envisioned, e-mail the file to your teacher for review, share it with your classroom colleagues, or submit it to an awards committee.

Adding a Talking Head

If you want to jazz up your presentation, you can switch to a headshot of yourself talking from time to time, or insert a small picture of yourself talking in the corner of each slide. Adding a headshot may help personalize the presentation, but we suggest keeping the focus on the slide information rather than your face. We are sure your face is pleasant to look at, but staring at a speaker for a long time can be tiresome. After a few minutes, the viewer will begin to focus more on your facial features, your haircut, or that almost-pimple beside your nose rather than the material you are presenting. And there can be a lag between your mouth moving and the audio of your words. However, a few brief headshots or a small insert can work fine. We will leave you to tackle how to insert such a file if you choose to do so.

What you should *never* do is sit in front of your computer or phone and read. Not much in academic life is more boring than watching someone read. Sure, we see that kind of thing at live conferences too, and it is never okay. For 99% of people, reading creates a monotonous rhythm with no spirit. In fact, we will go so far as to say do not even give a regular (nonread) presentation as a talking head on the screen. We know it seems easy to approach a presentation this way, and it is easy, but do not just open your computer or phone, sit at a table, and talk while the device records audio and video. Save the simple approach for Skyping friends and family who already love you.

Publishing 14

The Ultimate Presentation

N ow that you have a manuscript prepared—and hopefully you have even presented your work in some way—you might want to consider submitting the paper to a journal for possible publication. Here we cover some things to think about and steps to take toward publication.

Is Your Paper Worthy?

First, did you conduct a thorough review of the literature? Sometimes when you only have a limited time frame, such as one semester, it is difficult to be thorough. We know you read many articles in preparation for your presentation, but it is also likely that more delving into the literature would be worthwhile. You should read enough studies about your topic that you (1) learn what the general ideas and beliefs are in an area, then (2) learn that conflicting evidence exists. Students always seem annoyed when they read enough articles to find contradictory evidence, but of course there are at least two sides to every story, and a thorough researcher will find both.

Second, did you learn the methodology used in the area of interest? Of course you want to link your idea with research that already exists, so if a specific measure is generally used, you probably want to include it. Or if a construct is measured using a reliable and valid scale, include the same scale in your study. Hopefully you also thought about any variables that might get in the way of your study. These are generally called *confounding variables,* and you can learn more about these in another *EasyGuide* focused on design (Schwartz, B. M., Wilson, J. H., & Goff, D. M. [2015]. *An EasyGuide to Research Design & SPSS.* Thousand Oaks, CA: Sage).

Third, did you find significant results? Nonsignificant results can truly mean that two variables are not related to each other, but nonsignificance could also mean you ran a sloppy study. We assume that you would not run a messy study, but editors cannot know for sure. So although we hate to admit it, you most likely will not publish without significant results. And if you did find significant results, be sure to include effect sizes (again, the *EasyGuide* on statistics and design can help). Publishers often want to know not only if significant differences were found but also the details concerning those findings.

Fourth, is your writing clean and concise? Avoid passive voice; use active verbs as much as possible. Your overall paper organization should be smooth, and paragraphs should flow well with transitional words and phrases. Think of using transitions to take readers by the hand and lead them through your paper. Do not use fancy words when simple words will do. Avoid convoluted sentences. Be brief. And of course, avoid errors such as poor punctuation and misspelled words.

If you feel good about your paper, get a second opinion. Ask your instructor if your paper might be ready for publication. You do not want to waste your time, the professor's time, or the time and effort of an editor and reviewers if your paper is not of the caliber to be published. We are not trying to discourage you. We want you to publish. But a lot of honest input from others is helpful at this early stage of your career.

Journal Issues

When you and your instructor agree that you should submit your paper, go ahead and identify a journal. In fact, go ahead and identity two or three journals. You can look for a journal based on your topic or field, or you can focus on an undergraduate journal if you are an undergraduate student. Unfortunately, few undergraduate journals exist. Run a Google search to see if you can locate an undergraduate journal in your field (e.g., psychology), then look at the purpose of each journal. If you are a graduate student or an undergraduate with an outstanding paper, you can submit to a regular journal that publishes in your area. What does the journal publish? Look at a table of contents and maybe a sample paper or two. Get a feel for whether or not your paper is the type the journal accepts.

While examining journals, you might want to look at the rejection rate, usually defined as the percentage of submitted manuscripts that are rejected. An 80% rejection rate seems high but is a reasonable rejection rate because it reflects some poorly written papers, those with no significant results, and requested revisions that were never completed by authors. A couple of additional issues to consider are journal format and cost of publication. Format involves whether the journal is published in print form or internet-based only. Although some researchers prefer traditional printed journals, e-journals are gaining popularity. We have also noticed an increase in the number of journals requiring authors to pay publication costs. Perhaps this is also a growing trend, but paying for publications is not a practice we have embraced.

When you determine that a specific journal would make a good home for your paper, look at the "Instructions to Authors" to find out how your paper should be formatted. You will need to format the paper and references to suit the needs of the journal. We suggest talking with your instructor at any point in this process, but definitely talk with your teacher after you have identified an appropriate journal and formatted your paper. Your teacher can make sure you are on track and offer input on the final draft of your paper.

Most journals only accept online submissions at this point, beginning with you creating an account on their site. Next, you will enter details about yourself, including your school and contact information. You will also need a cover letter or at least a cover paragraph. We offer a letter as an example.

Dear (editor's name here),

The manuscript submitted here, *Student-Teacher Rapport Enhances Student Outcomes,* reveals a relationship between measures of rapport and student outcomes such as motivation, attitudes toward learning, and even students' final grades.

The body of the manuscript is 2,961 words, with 3 figures and 22 references. The manuscript is not under consideration elsewhere. We received IRB approval and treated all participants ethically.

We look forward to working with you and reviewers toward potential publication.

Respectfully submitted,

Janie H. Wilson, PhD

Submitting Your Manuscript

Go to the spot on the site where you "Submit a New Manuscript." There you will upload the paper. Usually a site offers you the chance to upload the body of the paper as well as figures and tables.

Somewhere in the submission process, you might be asked:

1. Did you receive IRB approval to run your study, and were participants treated ethically? If your answer is "no" to either of these, you should stop the submission process!

2. Is your paper being considered for publication elsewhere? If your answer is "yes," you should stop submitting.

3. What are the numbers of words, tables, figures, and perhaps references in your paper?

4. Did you removing all identifying information from the paper so reviewers can look over it without knowledge of the author(s)?

This practice, called a blind review, is useful to make sure the name of the author does not sway reviewers one way or the other. That is, a famous author might cause reviewers to be lenient and accept a manuscript without full consideration of merit. However, an author new to the field might be discriminated against because he or she has not published in the area previously. You can imagine other discriminations that might occur, including not wanting to publish the research of women or people indicated as potential minorities by their names. We would like to assume discrimination would never happen, but a blind review removes such a possibility.

After you upload all materials, the site will often build a pdf. document and ask you to review it before you officially submit it. Take a look to make sure everything looks okay, and then hit Submit. Usually you will immediately get an e-mail to confirm that the editor received the submission, and the e-mail will include your official manuscript number. Sometimes the e-mail will also say how long it might be before you hear back from the editor and reviewers. The general wait time is 3 months. It is acceptable to e-mail the editor and politely ask about the status of your manuscript after 3 months have passed. At that time, the editor should give you an update that includes how much longer you may have to wait for reviews. You decide if you want to leave the paper with the same journal or submit it elsewhere. We usually leave a manuscript where it is rather than begin the process all over again, but at 6 months with no end in sight, withdrawing a paper might be a reasonable option. To withdraw a paper, simply e-mail the editor to let him or her know that you are withdrawing. As always, be polite and respectful. Not only is a kind approach the best way to live life, you might decide to submit to that journal again in the future. Do not burn bridges.

Editorial Decisions

Let us imagine that after 3 months you receive an e-mail from the journal editor. You will hear one of three decisions:

1. Rejection—Which can include a thank-you message, a comment that the journal received a large number of submissions, a message that your paper did not fit well with the journal, or any number of other nice comments that pretty much send the same message: We will not be publishing your paper.

2. Revise and resubmit—Which means you have won the game . . . almost. A decision of revise and resubmit usually means the reviewers liked your paper. They saw merit in your work. Their positive opinion might be hard to spot when you read the

reviews because peers can be scathing in their comments. Keep in mind that you have been invited to continue the conversation with the editor and reviewers. They might want to see more data analysis, more explanation of findings, or so on. Consider whether or not you think you can address their comments. See the section below for exactly how to approach the task.

3. Accept—Which means you are one of the select few who do not have to continue a conversation with reviewers and the editor in order to get them to commit. You will (most likely) be published in the journal. In truth, we can almost guarantee that a few changes will be made prior to publication, but changes should be small and easy to accomplish. The authors of this textbook have published many times and have not experienced "Accept," only "Revise and Resubmit." We are not bitter. And we will not rest until we have earned at least one "Accept" of a manuscript.

With all three decisions, the editor will include a letter and usually provides comments from the reviewers. Reviewers' names are not included but instead are labeled as "reviewer A," "reviewer B," and so on.

So You Have Been Rejected

Dear Mr. James,

Thank you for your recent submission to the *Journal of All Things Wonderful*. We regret that we will be unable to publish your manuscript. The reviewers and I feel that your paper does not place your research in the context of a larger theory. See attached reviewers' comments.

We wish you continued progress in your research. Please consider submitting to our journal when you have future projects.

Yours truly,

Journal of All Things Wonderful Editorial Team

If you are rejected, you might be tempted to throw a tantrum, decide the editor is an idiot, or click your manuscript and data files to the Recycle Bin of your computer. Avoid these responses. You might feel compelled to e-mail the editor to say it is clear that the reviewers did not read your paper carefully because they missed key components. E-mailing a response to rejection is *not* acceptable. Such a practice would be like telling your boyfriend or girlfriend that you do not accept his or her breakup. If someone rejects you—in any way—walk away with dignity—no parting words, no redirection, and no begging to know why the rejection happened. Move on.

Give yourself a day or two to process the e-mail, if you would like. Then, if reviewer comments have been included in the e-mail, read them. Read them two or three times. Comments can be kind or rude, and the rude ones can really sting. No matter. Ignore the tone, and try to learn from the comments. One useful practice is to read the reviews twice, once to skim and the second time for details, then save the file to think about for a few days. For some of us, only after sleeping on the comments can we give them careful consideration. And the good news is that the reviews can strengthen the paper so that it might have a better chance of being published somewhere else.

Yes, that is right. When a paper is rejected, researchers do not give up. If you still believe in your paper, and the reviewers did not break your spirit by letting you know your manuscript is totally worthless, submit somewhere else. As a caution, start keeping a file of the title of your paper and where it was submitted so you do not accidentally submit to the same journal twice. After all, you may find yourself submitting your paper to several journals (never more than one at the same time) before finding a home for your work. We trust that each rejection and round of comments further improves the manuscript and increases the chance of publication.

Submit to a new journal using the same process outlined earlier. If you are rejected again, look for patterns in reviewers' comments. Perhaps reviewers keep saying that you should run more participants. If so, decide if you want to take some time to do that and reanalyze the larger data set. If reviewers want a more developed theory, talk with your teacher about ways to elaborate on the paper's introduction. You get the idea.

Revise and Resubmit: A Winning Combination

Dear Mr. Garcia,

Thank you for your recent submission to *Publishing Perfect Papers*. The reviewers and I find merit in your paper and would like to consider publishing your work pending acceptable revisions. The reviewers raised some interesting points that we would like you to consider and address. If you choose to revise your paper, the revision will be sent to reviewers. A decision of revise and resubmit does not guarantee publication; however, we look forward to receiving your revised manuscript.

If you choose to revise, please do so within the next 2 months. Clearly address all reviewer comments and suggestions in a detailed cover letter submitted with your revision. Refer to your manuscript number in all correspondence.

Sincerely,

Editor, *Publishing Perfect Papers*

This decision from an editor is usually the best an author can hope for. When we get this message, we celebrate. And we make sure we find that happy place in our hearts to enjoy before we open reviewers' comments and suggestions. Give yourself a moment to bask in the glory of potential acceptance. A decision of revise and resubmit is most definitely good news.

After you called your mom or dad or grandparents or children to brag and have posted the good news to Facebook or Twitter, read the reviewers' comments. Do not panic. Read them carefully, make notes, and talk with your instructor. Come up with a plan to address comments.

You will need to address the comments in two places: on the manuscript and in a reply letter. Some people like to start with the reply letter, where they can copy a specific comment or group of related comments, then say how they addressed the suggestions in the manuscript. If reviewers want many changes, the reply letter can be long. We think it is best to copy each suggestion followed by a narrative that addresses it. To make your organization obvious, perhaps bold each reviewer's comments and use a numbering system, or some other way to make the letter easy to follow. On the manuscript, of course make the changes you explained in the letter.

Dear (editor's name here),

Thank you for allowing me to revise my manuscript after reviewing comments and suggestions. Below is a detailed list of how reviewer comments were addressed within the paper. The revised manuscript is 2,341 words, with 2 figures and 18 references.

Reviewer #1
The author needs to hypothesize why student-teacher rapport did not impact grades.
Lack of effect on grades was addressed in the manuscript by explaining numerous sources of variability in the outcome of grades. Prior research suggests that grades are impacted by student motivation, number of classes missed, and student participation, to name a few additional variables.

Reviewer #2
This paper fails to offer key participant variables in the Method section.
Participant variables of gender, age, and ethnicity were added to the Method section. Given the potential impact of student major and class size, those variables were also summarized in the Method section.

I look forward to working with you and the reviewers to craft a publishable manuscript. Please let me know if further changes are needed.

Respectfully submitted,

Samantha Elias

As you read over the letter above, notice that changes were summarized. Details of the changes are located in the paper. You can even refer to a page number for each change if you would like. And be sure to incorporate new references in the paper as needed. For example, in the response to Reviewer #1, prior research was mentioned; therefore, detailed references to support the new information should be included in the paper.

If you can address most of the reviewer comments but disagree with one or two, you can make the case for why you disagree. Most people think they have to make all suggested changes, but remember that reviewers are giving you their input based on what they read. If you can offer additional support for your approach, they will listen. Sure, the editor and reviewers may still disagree with you, and you might still be required to make a specific change prior to official acceptance, but at that time, you can make your final decision about the change.

When you are invited to revise a manuscript, drop everything else and do it. Do not wait for the paper to get colder or your motivation to fade. When you are this close to a publication, you must make it your priority. You should also know that a quick revision usually means the same reviewers will see your paper a second time. Because they already liked it, you do want the same people. If you wait too long, your paper might be given to a new team of reviewers who might decide *not* to publish it. The bottom line is to revise as soon as you possibly can, but make sure your teacher has input, and be sure to proofread carefully.

If an editor and reviewers are happy with your manuscript, the editor will e-mail you. Usually the decision will come quickly, but you might have to wait another 3 months. Just as with the original submission, after 3 months you can e-mail the editor to ask for an update.

Dear Dr. Livingston,

We received your revised manuscript, and the reviewers agree that you addressed our concerns well. Thank you for your thorough attention to the comments and suggestions. Your paper will be published in the June edition of our journal; therefore, we will contact you to review page proofs in the near future.

At this time, we ask that you complete the attached publishing agreement and return it by fax or a .pdf e-mail attachment.

Sincerely,

Editorial Team

Notice in the e-mail above that the editor indicated when your paper will be published. This information will not always be given. Sometimes the editor does not know exactly when the paper will be in print. Within a day or two of receiving the e-mail, sign and return the publishing agreement and any other paperwork required by the journal.

Accepted

Really, what more is there to say? As the editor prepares your paper for journal publication, changes in formatting will likely happen, and you will be asked to review them. Or the editor and reviewers might ask for minor changes that should only take you a short time to accomplish. Remember what we said at the end of the prior section. All changes should be made immediately and returned to the journal as soon as possible. The editor might give you a deadline, but authors generally know that acceptance is golden and difficult to obtain, and one way to be grateful is to make those changes today!

Prior to publication, you will receive page proofs to review, make final changes, and accept as ready to publish. When you receive page proofs, you only have a couple of days to answer any remaining (very minor) questions from the editorial team and carefully proofread your entire article. It is exciting to see the final format of your article. At this point you are not allowed to make major changes, but a final read should still be completed to avoid embarrassing mistakes before they are forever in print.

Now you know. Work closely with your instructor to produce high-quality work and maneuver through the submission process. There is no guarantee that your manuscript will be accepted by a journal, but you should not give up easily. If rejected by a journal, carefully read reviewers' comments (if provided), revise your paper as needed, and submit to another journal. When peer experts offer critical evaluations of your manuscript, it truly does improve the final product.

We hope submitting a paper for potential publication is not as scary as it once was. Even though a lot of steps must be taken to publish, and the process takes time, successful publication means your work will be available to the entire world. We think you will agree that publication is the final goal of scholarly work. Publishing is the ultimate way to present your research.

Appendix A

Checklists for Posters and Oral Presentations

B elow we provide what you might call a "to-do" list for your presentation. Included are recommendations for preparing your presentation, traveling to a presentation, and even tasks to accomplish after your presentation.

Posters

_____ Check the conference website to know what size your poster should be for the conference. If the presentation is for a class, ask your instructor for poster size.

_____ Follow APA-style format for your figures and tables.

_____ Make sure the size of your text and figures are large enough to be read by anyone standing about 3 feet away from your poster.

_____ Determine that your poster content clearly and concisely communicates your research.

_____ Prepare a brief (a few minutes) talk to summarize your research to those interested in your poster.

_____ Be sure to include your contact information on your poster (e.g., in the lower right corner of your poster).

_____ Create handouts to give to those walking by or stopping to learn about your poster.

_____ Find out the cost of printing your poster at a professional print shop (or on campus if that resource is available). Decide on color versus black and white.

_____ Ask your instructor to review your poster.

_____ Summarize your poster for someone not familiar with your work.

_____ Proofread your poster carefully before taking it to the printer.

_____ For travel, purchase a mailing tube to protect and transport your poster to the conference.

_____ Bring along materials (e.g., tacks) needed to put your poster on the provided board.

_____ Find the location where you are assigned to set up your poster.

Oral Presentations

_____ Determine how much time you will have for your presentation.

_____ Identify what information can be included in your presentation given the time allotted.

_____ Develop slides for your presentation using appropriate software.

_____ Include notes on your slides, or write out notes to use during your talk (but _not_ read to your audience).

_____ Practice your talk out loud to determine the length.

_____ Practice again with an audience (e.g., a friend or your teacher).

_____ Practice again!

_____ Save copies of your talk to several locations.

For a Poster or Oral Presentation

_____ Identify a conference appropriate for your presentation.

_____ Read details at the conference website for information on submission guidelines, including deadlines, word limitations, and whether or not faculty sponsorship is required.

_____ Check on hotel accommodations if you are traveling to a conference away from home. The conference website will have information about hotels with conference rates.

_____ Decide how to travel to the conference. If you choose to fly, make arrangements to arrive no less than the day before your presentation.

_____ Check the conference website for information on when to register for the conference.

_____ Make sure you received information on when and where you will be presenting. This can usually be found on the conference website if the program is available online.

_____ Practice, practice, practice.

_____ Prepare answers for the questions you anticipate that others are likely to ask you.

_____ Pack appropriate conference attire. Pack your poster or electronic version of your talk.

_____ Practice, practice, practice.

_____ Get a good night's sleep the night before your presentation.

_____ Make good choices! Avoid late night parties and alcohol.

_____ Arrive 10 minutes prior to the start of your session.

_____ Within a few days after the conference, send your poster or paper to those who asked you to send information.

_____ Turn in all receipts in order to get reimbursed for any expenses covered by grants or your affiliated institution.

Carefully go through this checklist, and we guarantee you will be better prepared to give a professional presentation of your work. In fact, we will go ahead and congratulate you on completing this process in a highly organized way.

Appendix B

Assessment of Posters and Oral Presentations: Rubrics

If your poster or presentation is an assignment in a course, you will more than likely be graded on your work. If that is the case, as is true for most assignments, you want to make sure you clearly understand what is expected. How these expectations or guidelines are communicated differs from one class to the next. Sometimes you can find the details within the syllabus, where a calendar of assignments includes the details of information to include and what is expected.

What is more likely is that your instructor will provide some detail about the assignment in your syllabus but leave the information concerning what defines a good assignment for later in the term. At that point, we encourage you to ask your instructor if a rubric is available that clearly defines what is expected (and how your grade will be determined). Though rubrics are usually discussed in the context of grading an assignment after it is submitted, we strongly believe the rubric is a perfect mechanism for communicating to students how to develop and prepare for a presentation. For example, if you see that your presentation style is included in the assessment, you are more likely to focus on how you are going to communicate the information to the audience. If presentation style is not included on the rubric, and it appears that style will not be a component of the assessment, you are likely to spend much less time working on delivery and much more time on the content of your presentation.

If you are giving a poster or talk for a conference, you are not really concerned about grading and assessment (though some conferences do have competitions and awards). Regardless, you are preparing your work to present to professionals in the field, and we know you want to do a good job. You are likely to be working with a faculty member on the poster or talk, so feedback will be available before heading off to the conference. Before you even start developing your presentation, we advise you to ask a faculty member for a rubric that might guide you. The rubric can provide you with questions to ask yourself as you organize your poster or write your presentation. Would you earn high numbers on the rubric, or are changes needed to strengthen your presentation?

Though every rubric is a little different from the next, there are parts of a rubric that we can summarize for you. These general components exist for either a poster or oral presentation—or even a paper. The first thing you will notice in a rubric is the separate sections devoted to different parts of your work. For each section, the number of points you earn depends on the quality of your work. Quality is defined by how well your work meets the expectations as defined by your instructor on the rubric. In most cases, the more points you earn, the higher the quality of your work. The total points you earn is divided by the total number of possible points times 100, which determines your grade.

As you will see in the examples we include, rubric formats can vary widely, with different categories and different scores used. Some rubrics include scales that range from 0 to 4, and others include Likert-type scales that range from 1 to 5. In the end, no matter what the format or the scale, the point of the rubric is to assess your work.

The easiest way to understand a rubric is to see one. Take a look at the rubric on the next page. This rubric is used to assess a poster presentation. The second author uses the rubric when she includes a poster session in some of her lab courses. In this example, scores are calculated for different parts of the poster, including organization and appearance, and for the overall presentation style. Then for each category, the instructor assigns a score. In this example, low numbers represent weak sections, and high scores represent strong sections. Under each score, you will find a description of how a student earns those points. For example, if the abstract on a poster includes most information but is missing some key points, the student would likely earn a score of 3. Some rubrics include ranges of scores for each section (e.g., 1 to 3 points), and others, like the one on the next page, have a single point value for each category.

Rubrics for a Poster Presentation

In addition to looking over a rubric, consider asking your instructor for an example of a poster that received the highest number of points and one with a low score. The more detailed the assessment, the better. That way, you can understand what it means when a poster "clearly summarized the research" or "visual presentation was easy to read." If you are able to understand each component of the rubric, then you will be able to self-assess your project before getting feedback from peers or your instructor.

Category	1	2	3	4
Abstract	Abstract was not clearly connected to the research poster or presentation.	Abstract was somewhat connected to the research/presentation. Content of information was not sufficient.	Abstract adequately presented research, but more information would have been beneficial.	Abstract strongly represented the student's research and contained all the important information.
Content	Poster content did not connect with the purpose of the research, including the hypothesis, research question, method, conclusions, or implications.	Poster content somewhat conveyed a connection to the study, hypothesis, research question(s), method, conclusion, and/or implications.	Poster content adequately presented the content of the study, research hypothesis, or question(s) is somewhat general. Conclusion and implications were reasonable.	Poster content included material that clearly summarized the research. Material conveys the purpose of study, hypothesis, or research question. Strong conclusion and implications presented.
Appearance/ Clarity	Visual presentation was difficult to read and not effective.	Visual presentation was acceptable but needs improvement on use of space, fonts, colors, figures/tables, and headings.	Visual presentation was adequate but could use some refining on use of space, fonts, colors, figures/tables, and heading.	Visual presentation was easy to read and provided for an effective presentation. Good use of space, fonts, colors, figures/tables, and headings.
Organization	Structure of the presentation of material provided a very weak link between the information presented and topic of research.	Structure of presentation of material is somewhat confusing and topic of research difficult to follow.	Structure of material can be followed, but some refining would allow for clearer logic of presentation of research.	Structure of material is logical, and provides very clear information that connects your literature review, method, and conclusions.
Oral Component	Presenter was not prepared to discuss the research and did not convey an understanding of the research/poster content. Presenter's style of presentation lacked professionalism (e.g., eye contact). Unable to answer questions.	More practice was needed. Presenter was somewhat prepared to discuss the research, but did not convey a sense of confidence to provide an understanding of the different components of the poster (e.g., research problem, method, conclusion). Difficulty answering questions.	Preparation of presentation was acceptable, but some additional practice would have eliminated some issues with communicating the understanding of the research and the style of presentation, including answering questions.	Preparation of presentation was clear. Presenter clearly discussed the research, provided a professional discussion of the material, had excellent presentation style, and was able to answer most questions.

Poster Presentation Evaluation Form

Student Name: _____

Short Title: _____

Instructions. Please evaluate the seven major categories of the presentation using the 5-point scale provided.

LITERATURE REVIEW
(Circle one)

1	2	3	4	5
Low quality poster presentation		Average quality poster presentation		Highest quality poster presentation

Communicates research question(s) and relevance in a manner easy to understand; poses appropriate research question(s); discusses necessary, important previous research related to the research question.

METHOD
(Circle one)

1	2	3	4	5
Low quality poster presentation		Average quality poster presentation		Highest quality poster presentation

Uses methodology appropriate to research question; explains methodology so that reader can follow what was done in the study.

RESULTS
(Circle one)

1	2	3	4	5
Low quality poster presentation		Average quality poster presentation		Highest quality poster presentation

Uses the data analysis method most appropriate to the study; clearly presents the results of the data analysis; relates the data analysis results to the original research question(s).

DISCUSSION
(Circle one)

1	2	3	4	5
Low quality poster presentation		Average quality poster presentation		Highest quality poster presentation

Addresses theoretical implications of the research findings, if applicable; addresses implications of the research findings for meaningful future research; addresses any methodological limitations and/or confounding variables present in the study.

VISUAL PRESENTATION
(Circle one)

1	2	3	4	5
Low quality poster presentation		Average quality poster presentation		Highest quality poster presentation

Poster is organized in a sensible manner that is easy to follow; visual features of the poster (e.g., diagrams, graphs, charts, tables, text, figures) are easy to read and understand; proportion of textual to non-textual components is appropriate and enhances the reader's understanding of the project.

ACCOMPANYING VERBAL DESCRIPTION
(Circle one)

1	2	3	4	5
Low quality poster presentation		Average quality poster presentation		Highest quality poster presentation

Presentation is brief but informative (not just reading the poster content); presenter(s) uses vocal variety in rate and intensity to heighten and maintain interest; physical behaviors of the presenter(s) (e.g., eye contact, hand gestures, pacing) effectively support the presentation; Responds appropriately to issues and questions raised (If no relevant questions are asked, use only the other three items in this section as the basis for your numerical evaluation).

OVERALL RESEARCH QUALITY
(Circle one)

1	2	3	4	5
Low quality poster presentation		Average quality poster presentation		Highest quality poster presentation

The research question is valid and well formulated; the study actually tests the hypothesis/hypotheses; the research is well done overall (not just well presented research that is of low quality).

Rubrics can also include Likert-type scales with statements below each section that describe what aspect of the poster is under consideration. The following example illustrates a modified rubric from the Psychology Department at the University of Mary Washington.

Paper-Presentation Rubrics

Although presentation rubrics contain many of the same components (e.g., category of material assessed, points earned, and a brief description for each point), those for posters differ slightly from rubrics for oral presentations. Yes, there will be some overlap in what is included since the purpose of both is to convey information about your research. However, you know that a poster presentation is different from a paper presentation. We provide you with an example of two different paper-presentation rubrics. The first one uses a 5-point scale, with descriptions at the anchors (ends) and midpoint of the scale. This type of scale allows for greater precision. Someone can decide that the presentation for a given part of your talk really fell somewhere in between the high score and the middle score.

The rubric below contains scoring details for the different parts of your research included in your presentation, with subscale descriptions to help you understand how the category score was determined.

Ideas and Content

_____ 5 Presentation was clear, focused, and on the research topic; development of ideas clearly presented.

_____ 4

_____ 3 Presentation lacked focus at times in certain areas; development of ideas somewhat unclear; at times seemed off topic.

_____ 2

_____ 1 Presentation was very unclear; failed to address the topic/ purpose of the research.

Organization

_____ 5 Order of information made it easy to follow the presentation.

_____ 4

_____ 3 Order of presentation is unclear. Changes needed to present ideas in a way that makes sense to the audience.

_____ 2

_____ 1 Order of presentation was difficult to follow.

Voice

_____ 5 Presenter seemed relaxed and comfortable, using an appropriate pace and volume.

_____ 4

_____ 3 Presenter level of nervousness distracted from following the presentation; the pace and volume made the presentation difficult to follow at times.

_____ 2

_____ 1 Presenter level of nervousness, pace and volume, and general lack of comfort was very distracting, making it difficult to follow the content of the presentation.

Engagement

_____ 5 Presenter was personable and engaging, making eye contact with the audience.

_____ 4

_____ 3 Presenter attempted to engage the audience but at times did not make eye contact and read directly from notes.

_____ 2

_____ 1 Presenter did not attempt to engage audience; seemed unaware of the audience; failed to make eye contact.

Visual Aids

_____ 5 Visual aids were effective and improved presentation; appropriately supported/supplemented presentation of material.

_____ 4

_____ 3 Visual aids were only somewhat used effectively; lacked organization and/or appropriateness.

_____ 2

_____ 1 Visual aids were not used effectively; irrelevant information; errors on slides; disorganized; distracted from presentation of material.

Polish, Poise, Preparedness

_____ 5 Completely prepared and obviously rehearsed; free of errors.

_____ 4

_____ 3 Somewhat prepared; more rehearsal would have strengthened the presentation; some errors and/or mistakes included.

_____ 2

_____ 1 Not prepared; presentation was sloppy and disorganized with many errors.

The final rubric below provides scores for different aspects of an oral presentation. Some rubrics include the different parts of a research paper, which are scored separately. In this modified rubric from the Psychology Department at the University of Mary Washington, you will see scores not only for presentation style but also for introduction, method, results, and discussion sections. It is similar to the rubric used above for posters but also assesses oral-presentation components.

Oral Presentation Evaluation Form

Student Name: _____

Short Title: _____

INTRODUCTION
(Circle one)

1	2	3	4	5
Low quality oral presentation		Average quality oral presentation		Highest quality oral presentation

Communicates research question(s) and relevance in a manner easy to understand; poses appropriate research question(s); discusses necessary, important previous research related to the research question.

METHOD
(Circle one)

1	2	3	4	5
Low quality oral presentation		Average quality oral presentation		Highest quality oral presentation

Uses methodology appropriate to research question; explains methodology so that audience can follow what was done in the study.

RESULTS
(Circle one)

1	2	3	4	5
Low quality oral presentation		Average quality oral presentation		Highest quality oral presentation

Uses the data analysis method most appropriate to the study; clearly explains the results of the data analysis.

DISCUSSION
(Circle one)

1	2	3	4	5
Low quality oral presentation		Average quality oral presentation		Highest quality oral presentation

Discusses theoretical implications of the research findings, if applicable; discusses implications of the research findings for meaningful future research; addresses any methodological limitations and/or confounding variables present in the study; responds appropriately to issues and questions raised by the audience that are relevant to the study (if no relevant questions are asked, use only the other three items in this section as the basis for your numerical evaluation).

PROCESS OF PRESENTATION
(Circle one)

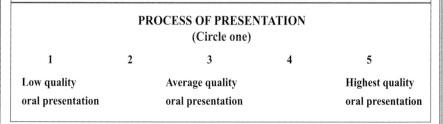

1	2	3	4	5
Low quality oral presentation		Average quality oral presentation		Highest quality oral presentation

Presentation is organized in a sensible manner that is easy to follow; presentation allocates appropriate amount of time for each of the main areas; presenter(s) uses vocal variety in rate and intensity to heighten and maintain interest; physical behaviors of the presenter(s) (e.g., eye contact, hand gestures, pacing) effectively support the presentation; visual features of the slide presentation (e.g., diagrams, graphs, charts, tables, text, figures) are easy to read and understand; slide presentation effectively supports and clarifies the oral presentation.

OVERALL RESEARCH QUALITY
(Circle one)

1	2	3	4	5
Low quality oral presentation		Average quality oral presentation		Highest quality oral presentation

The research question is valid and well formulated; the study actually tests the hypothesis/ hypotheses; the research is well done overall (not just well presented research that is of low quality).

Regardless of the rubric used to assess your work, each one provides the information that our students often ask us when preparing for any type of assignment. We know you have heard others in the class asking, "Will this be on the test?" Well essentially rubrics tell you exactly what will be on the test. They specify what a student should focus on when creating a poster or oral presentation. Use these rubrics. Ask yourself how you would score yourself on each section. Make any necessary changes, and score yourself again. Using the details from a rubric can improve your presentation by helping you focus on both content and style.

Index

⑤SAGE research**methods**

The essential online tool for researchers from the world's leading methods publisher

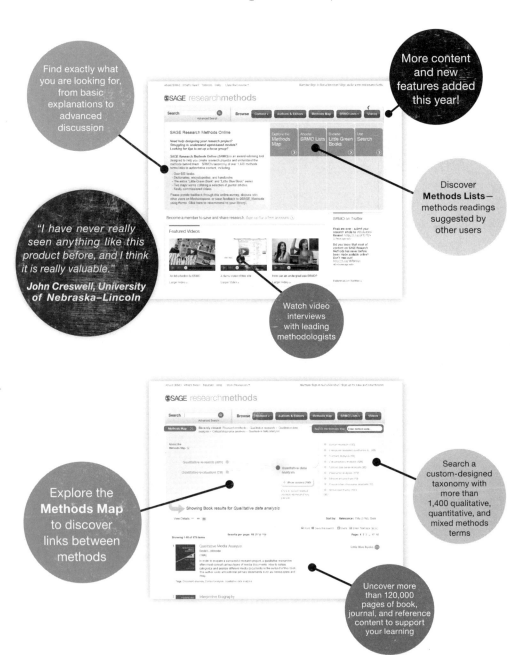

Find exactly what you are looking for, from basic explanations to advanced discussion

More content and new features added this year!

Discover **Methods Lists**— methods readings suggested by other users

"*I have never really seen anything like this product before, and I think it is really valuable.*"
John Creswell, University of Nebraska–Lincoln

Watch video interviews with leading methodologists

Explore the **Methods Map** to discover links between methods

Search a custom-designed taxonomy with more than 1,400 qualitative, quantitative, and mixed methods terms

Uncover more than 120,000 pages of book, journal, and reference content to support your learning

Find out more at
www.sageresearchmethods.com